Witnessing to Students

Christian Heritage Rediscovered

The Series, as the name suggests, is meant to focus on Christian Faith & Living vis-à-vis topics like Literature & Poetry, Indigenous Philosophizing, Ethical response towards Agriculture, Health & Healing, Science & Technology, Ecofeminist Theology, Sociological approach towards Human Rights, Law & Politics, Arts, History of Ideas, Ancient Civilizations, Cultural Contiguity, Religious Cosmologies & Mysticism, Footsteps of famous Theologians, World Peace & Harmony, Global Capitalism, Network Marketing, Cybertheology, Population & Demographics, Epigraphic Studies, Contextualized Education, and many others. We welcome a Mss. on any topic/s mentioned, whether they are original works, scholarly monographs, collections of conference papers, revised dissertations, or translations of historical documents. Through the Series we, the Publishers, are striving to put forward published works that may help Institutions, Academic Bodies, Researchers, Scholars and the World at large in furthering their respective knowledge and understanding on the concerned subject. We welcome your comments on our efforts and further suggestions on how we can foster the upcoming thoughtful theologically grounded books.

Christian Heritage Rediscovered - 16

Witnessing to Students
Efficacy of UESI in India

Potana Venkateswara Rao

Foreword by
Dr. Atul Y. Aghamkar

© Potana Venkateswara Rao

First Published in 2015 by

Christian World Imprints™
Christian Publishing & Books from India
H-12 Bali Nagar, **New Delhi-110015**
info@christianworldimprints.com
www.ChristianWorldImprints.com
Phone: +91 11 25465925 Fax: +91 11 25173055

ISBN-13: 978-93-5148-040-2 (HB)   ISBN-10: 93-5148-040-2 (HB)
ISBN-13: 978-93-5148-050-1 (PB)   ISBN-10: 93-5148-050-X (PB)

Cataloging in Publication Data--DK
Courtesy: D.K. Agencies (P) Ltd. <docinfo@dkagencies.com>

Venkateswara Rao, Potana, 1974- author.
Witnessing to students : efficacy of UESI in India / Potana Venkateswara Rao ; foreword by Dr. Atul Y. Aghamkar.
  pages   cm. -- (Christian heritage rediscovered ; 16)
Includes index.
ISBN 9789351480402 (HB)
ISBN 9789351480501 (PB)

1. Union of Evangelical Students of India. 2. Evangelistic work--India. 3. College students in missionary work. 4. Church work with minorities--India.   I. Title. II. Series: Christian heritage rediscovered ; 16.

DDC 269.20954   23

All rights are reserved. No part of this publication can be reproduced, distributed, performed, publicly displayed, stored in a retrieval system, made into a derivative work, transmitted or utilized in any form or by any means; electronic, mechanical, photocopying, recording or any information storage system, without the prior written permission of the copyright holder(s), as indicated, and the publishers.

Jurisdiction: Any conflict or dispute in relation to this publication shall be adjudged in accordance with the laws of India and the matter shall be subject to the jurisdiction of the Courts, Tribunals or any other Forums of New Delhi, India, only.

Disclaimer: The views and contents of this publication are solely of the Author(s); the Publisher may not subscribe to them.

Printed at Chawla Offset Printers

Dedicated

To my dear wife Rita Rao,
who is behind me in every success.
My lovely kids Sophia, Lydia & Ashish
whose presence refreshes me,
in times of trouble.

The Book

The significant feature about India is that it has "a wide variety of religious traditions." The Christian missions among these traditions face a great challenge. One of the observations in Indian missions is that the church has made a significant impact on *dalits* and *tribals*, but its impact on Hindu and the Muslim communities is insignificant.

The 'Union of Evangelical Students of India', popularly known as UESI, has been one of the prominent ministries contributing to this end. This book meticulously evaluates the modus operandi employed by this ministry for the attainment of this objective.

IVCF

With a strong combination of academic as well as practical research, Author provides a wealth of information with regard to how to do effective students' ministry in India. It also reflects Author's wide experience, insights and passion for the work of evangelization. The book is meant to seek answers of some unanswered questions like: Why Christian missions in India had been stagnated among the Dalits and Tribals only? Why they are not able to succeed in witnessing the Gospel to upper caste Hindus and Muslims also?

This factual and figurative presentation is going to be a manual for all those who passionately follow the teachings of Lord Jesus Christ and want to share the Gospel not only to the large student population of India but also meaningfully to the South Asian individuals and communities with relevance and sensitivity so that they could undergo a spiritual rebirth and pave their way towards revealing the Divine.

The Author

Sri Potana Venkateswara Rao, who is known as Bhakta Potana, is basically from Andhra Pradesh. He did his graduation in English literature from Acharya Nagarjuna University and also earned Masters in Social Work from the same University. He is also MA in Religion & Philosophy from Madurai Kamaraj University. Apart from this academic education, he is dedicated for spiritual education. He did his Master of *Divinity* from GFA Seminary, Tiruvalla, Kerala. He also did his theological research program Master of Theology from Union Biblical Seminary, Pune. At present, he is doing his PhD Research with the University of Mysore through South Asia Institute of Advanced Christian Studies (SAIACS). He lives in Bangalore with his wife Rita and three kids Sophia, Lydia & Ashish Vidwan.

Bhakta has been teaching God's word to the university students in India. His three years (1993-1996) as a student leader and eleven years (2000-2011) as a full time staff, in association with Union of Evangelical Students of India (UESI) opened opportunities to impact college and university students of both South and North India. He is not only an academician but he is a man on the *Mission* field who is down to earth.

Foreword

As per the 2001 Census of India, population age 15-24 years accounts for 195 million of the 1,029 million of India's population. In other words, every fifth person in India belongs to the age group of 15-24 years. These figures should compel Christians to get seriously involved in reaching this age group people as they are one of the most open, accessible and to a certain extent receptive group. The Union of Evangelical Students of India popularly known as UESI has been one of the prominent ministries that have hugely impacted the young student population of India. Potana Venkateswara Rao was a fruit of this ministry who was strategically used by God in Hyderabad and beyond to bring a number of students into the Kingdom of God.

This study reflects Potana's wide experience, insights and passion for students' ministry. Although academically oriented, it provides significant insights for effective student's ministry, especially among the upper castes Hindus and Muslims. With a strong combination of academic as well as practical research, Potana provides a wealth of information with regard to how to do effective students ministry in India. I have known him for a number of years, both as my student and teaching assistant, and I have observed his deep commitment for the cause of mission and evangelism in India. I heartily welcome this book and commend it to all who have passion to reach the student population of India.

Dr. Atul Y. Aghamkar
Professor of Missiology, SAIACS, India

Preface

Why Christians are so much concerned for the needy and for the transformation of the individuals and society?
This question had been in my mind from my college days. When I went to the university education in 1993, I have seen the role models of Christian lecturers and other professionals who demonstrated their love for the needy students in the city of Tenali, Andhra Pradesh. My interaction with Christian community in that city opened my eyes which helped me to see the genuineness of love and sacrificial service in day to day life of Christians. I had a great desire to become a social activist who can stand for the cause of the poor and the marginalized sections of the society. Fortunately, I became a field staff of Union of Evangelical Students of India (UESI) in the year 2000. My fourteen years: three years (1993-1996) as a student leader and eleven years (2000-2011) as a full time staff, of UESI opened opportunities for me to serve college and university students of both South and North India. During this period, I had the opportunity to interact with several Christian mission agencies and NGOs that are working in different parts of the country. Some of the indigenous Christian mission agencies are actively involved in spiritual liberation and transformation of the societies. More than ever the post independent Indian Christians have been making a great impact on serving the society. My observations in the field and interaction with the people made me think on several questions.

Why Christian missions in India had been stagnated among the dalits and tribals? Why they are not able to succeed in witnessing the Gospel to high caste Hindus and Muslims? I started reading and reflecting on these questions.

Preface

Mission history helps us to understand that there was an outcry for 'evangelizing the world in this generation' in World Missionary Council of Edinburgh in 1910. This evangelistic thrust and passion motivated and inspired young western missionaries to move to India with a view to evangelize the nation. In fact, Gospel came to India in three phases. The first phase of Evangelism in India was by St. Thomas in the first century. This phase of evangelism gave priority to witness the high caste Hindus especially in the State of Kerala. The second phase of evangelism was by Catholic mission that gave priority to witness many castes. The third phase of evangelism was by protestant Evangelicals who did not succeed in witnessing the high-caste Hindus that eventually made them to concentrate on harijans/dalits, tribals and rural folk. Since the western missionaries were passionate for numbers and numerical growth, they left the legacy of church growth among the marginalized sections of India because they turned to Christian faith as masses. The post-independent Indian evangelicals adapted and gave priority to numerical growth and concentrated on winning the winnable, the rural folk who belong to tribals and dalits. As a result, Indian missions neglected high caste Hindus and Muslims. The denominational missions that were initiated by the western missionaries, the evangelical Para-church ministries and indigenous evangelical mission agencies concentrated on evangelizing the marginalized sections of people of India while neglecting the Hindus and Muslims.

As a Bhakta of Christ, I have a great respect and love for India. My desire and love for Hindus and Muslims motivated me to do this research which enlightened me with many facts and figures. This research helped me to understand some of my unanswered questions and I am sure that it will answer some of your questions too.

I pray that this book will be a great blessing for Churches, Missions and Students of Missions in and outside India.

Bhakta Potana   09/02/2014
Bangalore

Acknowledgements

My heart is filled with gratitude to the Lord Christ Jesus, for His grace which alone has enabled me to complete this research work. I am grateful to my research guide.

Dr. Frampton Frank Fox, for his hard labor and investment in my two years of stay in Union Biblical Seminary, Pune. He has prepared me not only to write academic research book like this, but to face unwritten curriculum in life and ministry.

I acknowledge my loving parents, Nancharaiah & Manikyala Devi, and my brother, Srinivasa Rao, whose prayers and blessings are always with me to succeed in my pursuit of excellence.

I am thankful to Dr. David Jaya Kumar, General Secretary of UESI from 2005-2010, who graciously supported me to get the study leave for this research. My heartfelt thanks go to Mr. Emmanuel Subhakar, who has been used by God as a facilitator for my financial expenditure for this research.

I also acknowledge EU, EGF & Staff of UESI, who have helped me in different aspects of my research to complete this work.

Finally, I am extremely grateful to Mrs. & Dr. Montagu Barker who have been a great source of encouragement and of their presence on UBS campus has helped us to feel warmth of love and acceptance.

Contents

Foreword ix
Preface x
Acknowledgements xii

Chapter One: Introduction 1
   1.1 Statement of the Problem 2
   1.2 Elaboration of the Problem 2
   1.3 Purpose of the Study 3
   1.4 Definition of Key Terms 4
   1.5 Limitations 4
   1.6 Delimitations 4
   1.7 Research Questions 5
   1.8 Previous Research 5
   1.9 Methodology 5
   1.10 Outline of the Thesis 8

Chapter Two: Review of Relevant Literature 11
   2.1 History of UESI Ministry 12
   2.2 General Approaches to Ministry among Different Faiths . . 13
   2.3 Ministry among Muslims 17
   2.4 Ministry among Hindus 26
   2.5 Ministry to the Students in the Campuses 34

Chapter Three: Analysis and Interpretation of Data 43
   3.1   Ministry methods of UESI 44
   3.2   Response towards the Gospel from
          Students of different Faiths 52
   3.3   Mission among Students of different Faiths. 57
   3.4   Hindrances, Effective methods and
          Strategies to reach the Students of all Faiths 77

Chapter Four: Recommendations and Conclusions 89
   4.1   Theological/Biblical Reflection 89
   4.2   Recommendations from the
          Research Questions 91
   4.3   Recommendation for further research. 98

Index 112

Chapter One

Introduction

The significant feature about India is that it has "a wide variety of religious traditions."[1] The Christian mission among these traditions faces a great challenge. One of the observations in Indian missions is that the church has made a significant impact on *dalits* and *tribals*, but its impact on Hindu and the Muslim communities is insignificant. Hinduism has been arising as an emerging force to impact the world. In this connection Paul G. Hiebert reminds us that "we must recognize the impact of Hinduism on the rest of the world."[2] In fact, Hindu theology and practice is controlled by high-caste Hindus. Even though high-caste Hindus are a minority in Indian population, they have been dominating the social, religious and political conditions in India. The church in India faces the challenge of making an impact on Hindu society.

Another significant aspect about India is that it "has a Muslim population of some 150 million, making it the state with the second-largest Muslim population in the world after Indonesia."[3] Most of the Muslim nations are closed to the Gospel and it is very difficult to reach them; but Muslims are at our doorstep in India, where there is freedom to reach out to them.

It is a great challenge for the church in India to make an impact on the Hindu and Muslim communities by spreading the Gospel among them, because these communities are among the most influential communities in the world. The only hope of making an impact on them lies in concentrating on the young generations of these faith communities, because young people are more open to the Gospel and "they do not bind themselves into the blind beliefs. They ask questions and do not accept what does not satisfy their rational thinking."[4] Young people, especially college students, are more open to the Gospel because they think rationally and evaluate the truth. Another significant prediction by A. P. J. Abdul Kalam, is that "there is likely to be a large population of young people with aspirations of better lifestyle" by the year 2020.[5] In fact, if we observe the Indian population, "More than 50% of the population is less than 25 years of age and strong growth is expected to continue in this age bracket."[6] These young people, especially university students, are playing a vital role in Indian society. These people need to be transformed if India is to be transformed, because the future of India is in their hands. In this context, this study is an attempt to understand the impact that the Union of Evangelical Students of India (UESI) has on students of different faiths with an intention to help the movement's efforts to focus on Hindu and Muslim students.

1.1 Statement of the Problem

This research is an evaluation of UESI's mission to Christian, Hindu and Muslim students of Hyderabad so that UESI and other campus ministries may improve their ministry to students of all faiths.

1.2 Elaboration of the Problem

A small prayer group for college students, conducted every Friday evening in Prof. H. Enoch's residence in Madras, gave birth to UESI on 18 September 1954.[7] It is also known as the Evangelical Union (EU) throughout the country and is recognized for its excellence in raising spiritual leadership. This is an interdenominational student movement affiliated to the International Fellowship of Evangelical Students and its main areas of focus are evangelism, fellowship, testimony and missions. Its vision statement says, "UESI seeks to evangelize post-matric students in India and nurture them as disciples of the Lord Jesus Christ so that they may serve the Church and Society."[8] One of the great strengths of UESI is that it has a task force of three levels. The first level comprises student believers who lead the ministry, the second level are professionals who mentor these student groups and the third level is made up of full-time staff who shepherd both the students and the professionals. Thus, UESI has made a great impact on the country by witnessing to students in all the states. Although UESI has a long history, its impact on high-caste Hindu and Muslim students is low. It seems that its ministry is mostly prevalent among students of Christian background.

1.3 Purpose of the Study

The Indian Church's contribution to high-caste Hindus and Muslims is very low. It concentrates its efforts mostly among nominal Christians, Scheduled Castes and Scheduled Tribes, while neglecting high-caste Hindus and Muslims. In this context, I have chosen to focus on the UESI in order to understand its impact on students from Christian, Hindu and Muslim backgrounds. My major concern is to explore its mission among students of different faiths. My focus is to encourage the UESI to reach out to high-caste Hindus and Muslims.

The reason behind selecting the UESI is that student movements in the past have made a significant impact in world evangelization and have been behind the formation of mission agencies. The UESI has also played a vital role in Indian missions and its contribution to raising leadership within the Indian church is significant. Quite a number of leaders and staff belonging to prominent mission agencies such as the Indian Evangelical Mission (IEM), Friends Missionary Prayer Band (FMPB), World Vision, INTERSERVE INDIA, and Evangelical Field of ... (EFICOR) have an UESI background. David Jaya Kumar found that "The Indian Evangelical Mission had about 70-80 percent missionaries from UESI affiliates."[9] In fact, UESI has the potential to make an impact on the largely untouched high-caste Hindus and Muslims, which is why I want to encourage the movement to turn their efforts in this direction.

1.4 Definition of Key Terms

Some of the technical terms and words that I have used in this research need to be clarified. The word "mission" is used in the title of the thesis itself in the context of evangelism. In the context of missiology the word "mission" may mean many things, but I have used this term only in the context of evangelism. The word "added" is used to denote those who have recently accepted Jesus Christ as their personal savior and joined the group. The words "reach" and "reaching" are used to indicate "evangelizing the students." "Students of different faiths" mean students who come from Christian, Hindu and Muslim backgrounds. The other technical terms are clarified wherever clarification is needed.

1.5 Limitations

This research is limited to the UESI ministry within the city of Hyderabad. UESI has a huge network in India because it has been working in all the states. The research is limited to universities in Hyderabad and it is not a comparative study of other youth and student movements. The literature on reaching Indian students is nil. There are a few books written in the context of youth ministry, but I did not find relevant literature in the context of reaching students and, in fact, nothing was written on reaching high-caste Hindu students and Muslim students. This is one of the major limitations in reviewing the literature. Another limitation is that there may be students from other faith backgrounds—such as Buddhist, Sikh and Jain—but my focus is on missionary activity among Christian, Hindu and Muslim students.

1.6 Delimitations

The research covered the impact of UESI on students belonging to different faiths in major Universities in Hyderabad such as Central University of Hyderabad (HCU), Osmania University (OU), Jawaharlal Nehru Technical University (JNTU) and Acharya NG Ranga Agricultural University (ANGAU). Since the UESI ministry in Hyderabad is flourishing and strong among the university students, it was easy for me to collect a good number of questionnaires and conduct interviews from the key leaders of the movement which is an advantage for my research. Another factor is that I am very familiar with the place and people who are active in the ministry of UESI in Hyderabad. An additional reason for selecting Hyderabad is that it is a city with Hindu, Muslim, and Christian students, which is why my focus was on this city to have an effective evaluation of UESI's impact on different faiths.

1.7 Research Questions

There are four Research Questions (RQs) designed to investigate the subject, but each RQ has three angles of investigation. Each RQ deals with the UESI ministry among Christian, Hindu and Muslim students. In particular, RQ3 covers quite a large area of interest in which the major focus of the research is included.

RQ1. What are the methods UESI employs in Hyderabad universities in its ministry among Christian, Hindu and Muslim students?

RQ2. What is the response of the students from these three faiths towards the Gospel?

RQ3. What is the impact of UESI on the students of these three faiths?

RQ4. What strategies and implementation plans would help this organization evolve a better ministry among students of all three faiths?

1.8 Previous Research

There is some research on witnessing to Hindus and Muslims in a general sense but, as far as I know, there is no study on mission among students of different faiths. Other parallel areas of research will be surveyed in Chapter Two.

1.9 Methodology

This study comprises basically "empirical" research. Primary and secondary sources were used in this research. In the second chapter, library books and journals were extensively used to create a theoretical framework. A set of structured and well-prepared questionnaires and interviews were used to get accurate information from the field and some documents from UESI were collected and used in the presentation of the data.

1.9.1 Sampling

I have strategically selected samples with the help of key UESI leaders in Andhra Pradesh. Only mature believers who are members of UESI and those who are acquainted with the UESI ministry in Hyderabad were selected as sources of factual information.

Table 1: Frequency and the Percentage of the Questionnaire

Members	No. of Respondents	Percentage
EU Students	53	44%
EU Leaders	7	6%
EGF Members	20	17%
EGF Leaders	18	15%
Full-time Staff	6	5%
Not Revealed	16	13%
Total	**120**	**100%**

Table 2: Gender Ratios of the Respondents to the Questionnaire

Gender	No. of Respondents	Percentage
Male	96	86%
Female	21	17.5%
Not Answered	3	2.5%
Total	**120**	**100%**

Table 3: Interview Sample

Particulars	No. of Interviewed	Percentage
Full-time Staff of UESI	5	11%
Student Leaders (EU) who are involved in the ministry	19	42%
Professionals (EGF) who are involved in the ministry	21	47%
Total (44 male & 1 Female)	**45**	**100%**

1.9.2 Data Collection

Initially, I informed the key UESI leaders that I was selecting a research title that required adequate information from UESI members in Hyderabad. A well-prepared questionnaire was ready by April 2008. A soft copy of this questionnaire was sent through e-mail to most UESI members in Hyderabad as well as in the rest of Andhra Pradesh through the help of Yahoo group mail ids. Since most UESI members, especially the key leaders, are in these yahoo groups, most of them received the soft copy of my questionnaire well in advance. A pilot test was conducted with 4 people in UBS who belong to the UESI staff. This pilot test helped me identify difficult questions.

I travelled directly to Hyderabad from UBS during the summer vacation in April 2008. I selected a few key leaders who came forward to help me collect the data. Four hundred hard copies of the questionnaire were handed over to the EU, EGF and a few UESI staff with the help of volunteers. We handed over these questionnaires to the members of important Bible study groups in different university hostels, summer Leadership Training Camps and EGF Bible Studies where mature students and graduate leaders gather for fellowship.

I reached Hyderabad on 21st April 2008 and made appointments with key leaders to interview them. Since some of the important EU and EGF members who were well acquainted with the Hyderabad UESI ministry were scattered in other cities due to course completions and transfers, I had to travel to Warangal, Guntur, Vijayawada, Vishakapatnam and Vizianagaram to conduct interviews. Summer leadership camps in these places made it easy for me to get key leaders for interviews. Since most of the key leaders were well aware of my research they gave me a warm welcome and some of the busy people were willing to be interviewed even at late hours. I stayed at least one or two days in each university campus, where I conducted interviews with EU student leaders. Even though I initially planned to conduct only 35 interviews, I conducted 45 interviews due to the genuine interest and willingness to cooperate on the part of UESI leaders. All the interviews were conducted in English except with one Muslim student, Pasha, who preferred Urdu in which he was fluent.

I collected 89 completed questionnaires out of four hundred from the members while I was in Hyderabad from 21st April to 31st

May. Apart from the few days that I spent traveling to other cities, I spent most of the time in Hyderabad. A few student and graduate leaders took the responsibility of collecting and sending me the rest of the questionnaires, but I got only 31 more by post in November 2008. Thus, I could collect only 120 questionnaires from the field.

Another primary source was UESI documents, magazines and newsletters. I visited the UESI-AP office, which is located at Number (near Guntur) and spent a day collecting the relevant documents. A few documents and newsletters were collected from UESI's Hyderabad office.

1.9.3 Data Processing

The collected data was studied and tabulated from the questionnaires. Systematic and logical tables and figures were organized from the tabulation of the questionnaires. Valuable statements and information from the interviews were added to interpret the tables and figures.

1.9.4 Library Research

The library research method was used to understand what people have written in connection with my topic (Mission among students of different faiths with special reference to the approach of the Union of Evangelical Students of India in Hyderabad Universities) and to create a theoretical framework to analyze the field data in the light of what people have already written on this subject. Online journals from ATLA and books related to this title were identified in the library of the Union Biblical Seminary (UBS). The other libraries I drew upon in the city of Pune were Papal Seminary, Iswani Kendra and Neighbor Ministry (YWAM).

1.10 Outline of the Thesis

Chapter One deals with the introduction of the study, which includes the problem statement and related explanation, the purpose of the study, definitions, limitations, delimitations and a detailed description of the research methodology. Chapter Two covers the review of the literature related to the research topic. Chapter Three presents the data collected from the field in a logical and systematic manner to answer the RQs and it is the most important chapter as far as the research is concerned. The final chapter presents the conclusions that were derived from the interpretation of the data and makes recommendations.

Chapter Two

Review of Relevant Literature

Introduction

This chapter outlines the background for the research questions and for the field research. It reviews the available literature that provides a theoretical framework to evaluate and answer the research questions. The main thrust and focus of this research is to find out the impact of the UESI on students of Hindu, Christian and Muslim backgrounds. Scholars have written a lot on ministry to people of other faiths in a general sense, but research and scholarly literature on ministry to students of other faiths is lacking. In this context, I looked into scholarly literature that focuses on ministry to people of other faiths, especially to Hindus and Muslims and I tried to relate those theoretical and practical frameworks to the context of student ministry. Thus, in this chapter, I review the literature that deals with the theory and practice of Christian witness to Hindus and Muslims in a general sense to apply them to student ministry.

A brief history of the UESI is outlined in the first section to help the readers understand the background of the movement.

The following sections talk about general approaches to ministry among different faiths, in which the approach of contextualization is highlighted, and also different theories and practices of Christian witness to Muslims, Hindus and students on campuses. Since relevant material written by Indian authors in the Indian context is lacking, most of the sources referred to in this chapter are written by Western authors in their context, but they can be applied to the Indian context.

2.1 History of UESI Ministry

UESI is an indigenous student movement in origin, but its function and roots go back to western student movements such as the Student Christian Movement (SCM), and International Fellowship of Evangelical Students (IFES). Professor Enoch, a Zoology teacher in Visakhapatnam, Andhra Pradesh, was the initiator and one of the founding fathers of this student movement. He was an active member in SCM during his early days, but he was disappointed by the liberal thinking on Scripture and the overemphasis on social work while neglecting "the need for personal salvation and the fact that the Bible is the Word of God."[10] His efforts to influence the SCM to preserve evangelical thinking did not work. He left the SCM to stand for his evangelical convictions and was instrumental in forming the Inter-Collegiate Evangelical Union (ICEU) in Madras. He was passionate in his evangelical convictions and closely associated with Bro. Bakht Singh.

In the early 1950s, some of the student members of the SCM in Vellore left it due to its liberal thinking and "those who left the SCM had a great longing to start a witnessing evangelical group."[11] In fact, "the 1950s was a time for growth and expansion of campus ministry. It was also a time for new student organizations to represent the church on campus."[12] The Spirit of the Lord started working in different countries in different ways to meet the spiritual needs of the students. Especially in India, students with evangelical convictions started witnessing and were actively involved in evangelistic activities in the early 1950s. Likewise, there was another ICEU formed by H. S. Ponnuraj in Coimbatore in 1952. It was in 1954 that these three ICEU leaders of Madras, Vellore and Coimbatore came together and "finally, the Union of Evangelical Students of India was agreed upon, to distinguish this from other student movements in India and to underline the indigenous origin of the movement."[13] The movement spread rapidly to almost all the states in India with a vision "to evangelize post-matric students in India, nurture them as disciples of the Lord Jesus Christ, that they may serve the Church and society."[14] Its impact in the country is immeasurable and, in fact, "as the UESI continued its ministry over the last fifty years it has grown organizationally, structurally and in its ministry, beyond all expectations."[15] Its impact on the church, missions and society is noteworthy.

David Jaya Kumar, the present General Secretary of UESI, reports that "more than 500 camps are held in UESI ministry itself every year."[16] In almost all the camps and programs, the lay leaders and staff of UESI speak and train students of different faiths. Its impact on students belonging to different faiths is significant. In order to understand the impact of the UESI on students of different faiths in Indian campuses, the relevant literature on ministry to other faiths is reviewed in the following sections.

2.2 General Approaches to Ministry among Different Faiths

Christianity in India has a rich heritage because the Gospel came to the country in the first century itself. Attempts were made to reach high-caste Hindus by Catholic as well as Protestant missionaries, but some of the missionaries in the past (and even in the present) failed to understand the culture of the people of other faiths in their mission approach. Most of the Western missionaries had a negative attitude toward other faiths and so failed to develop contextual approaches to relate with people of other faiths in the Indian multi-religious and cultural context. In this context, this section mainly focuses on the theory and practices of Christian missions in their encounter with other religions in a general sense to draw some principles for an effective ministry to students of other faiths.

2.2.1 Early Missionaries' Ministry Approach to other Faiths

Some Christian missionaries in the past viewed non-western cultures as inferior to western culture. In fact, they did not see the distinction between culture and religion, but held that "culture is essentially a religious act."[17] In this connection, Ariarajah rightly pointed out that "the early missionary movement did not see the encounter of the Gospel to be with the cultures of other peoples, but with their religions."[18] Culture is interpreted in the light of civilization. Western culture was identified as civilized and other cultures were labeled as uncivilized. Also, "the Western Churches assumed that they had the best culture and the Gospel must be proclaimed to every nation in the Western cultural forms."[19] David points out that "Christianity as well as Western Civilization was promoted as superior to the religions and cultures of India."[20] Indian elite thinkers were upset with Christian mission work in India "because of the missionaries' abuse of other faiths and especially Hinduism and also because of the changes that came to settle on a convert."[21] Christianity was identified as the religion of the West because some of "the British officials during the first half of the 19th century tacitly and at times openly supported the missionary work as Christianity was also the religion of the rulers."[22] The Christian faith did not grow in the Indian culture in a way that it could make a significant impact on Hindu society.

Elite Indian thinkers "rejected Christianity because it was alien to the spirit and life of the people of India and it was considered to be an ally of Western Imperialism."[23] Even though some of the Western missionaries tried to assimilate into local cultures, they failed to relate to them meaningfully. The significant observation is that "Christianity propagated by the foreign missionaries was branded as a denationalizing force and the Indian Christians as agents of British Imperialism."[24] Indian Christians were always suspected by nationalistic leaders. "It was taken for granted that Britain had the full knowledge and power that others did not have. This assumption led them to colonize countries and annex them as their own."[25] Western civilization and knowledge was considered superior to all others.

Alexander Duff held the same theory, which may help us understand the spirit behind missionary work. In fact, he strongly believed that "British rule in India was understood as God's dispensation to prepare and enable India to receive Christianity."[26] Because of this conviction, some of the missionaries in India overlooked other religions and they had a confrontational attitude towards people of other faiths. The early missionaries' attitude towards other religions hindered mission work by preventing it from being relevant to the religiously pluralistic Indian context. In order to minister to students of different faiths, contextualization of the Gospel is the need of the hour—an enterprise neglected by the early missionaries.

2.2.2 Contextualization: An Approach to Relate with other Faiths

The concept of contextualization is much heard in recent mission practice. In fact, "Contextualization of the Gospel is not a recent phenomenon, but exists from the time God planned to maintain a relationship with human beings. But, the emphasis on the term 'contextualization' as a model of cross-cultural mission has been developed recently."[27] In 1970-71, the Theological Education Fund (TEF) popularized this theory in missionary practice. It is an umbrella-term that "includes indigenization of mission methods and theology."[28] In fact, indigenization is a part of contextualization. Contextualization of the Gospel is essential in our mission practice because contextualization "attempts to communicate the Gospel in word and deed and to establish the church in ways that make sense to people within their local cultural context, presenting Christianity in such a way that it meets people's deepest needs and penetrates their worldview, thus allowing them to follow Christ and remain within their own culture."[29] There is a great need for contextualization in our mission practice, especially to reach university students who belong to other faiths.

Christian missionaries have long been using the theory of contextualization in their mission practice. Parshall explains it in a simple way, saying that the "basic principle was to start where the person was in his own orientation to life."[30] The mission method of contextualization helps the missionary to assimilate into the local cultures, to understand them from their point of view. In the context of outreach to Muslims, "the American Phil Parshall, who was a missionary in Bangladesh and in the Philippines with Serving in Mission (SIM), played an important role in popularizing the theme through his many publications calling for contextualizing of the Gospel into the cultures of Islam."[31] Some Indian Christian thinkers from Hindu backgrounds like Sadhu Sunder Singh, Upadhyaya, Dayanand Bharati, and R.C. Das proposed and practiced contextual approaches in their mission practice among Hindus but there is no history that identifies these contextual models as practiced among Hindu and Muslim students in Indian campuses.

The main theory behind contextualization is to be relevant to people of different faiths and cultures. University students who belong to different faiths hold their own cultural and religious values and worldviews; in order to understand them better, Christian workers should stand in their shoes—in other words, practice contextualized ministry.

There are different methods that can be followed in the contextualization of the Gospel. Paul G. Hiebert talks about three types of methods in relating with people of different cultures.

The first method is denying the old cultural practices and beliefs which he calls "rejection of contextualization." Instead of adopting local cultural practices which go along with Biblical values, some missionaries in the past overthrew them. "For example, missionaries in India rejected red saris for brides, for this was the color worn by Hindus. Instead, they introduced white saris to symbolize purity, not realizing that in India red stands for fertility and white for barrenness and death."[32] Local cultures and religious beliefs and practices were considered evil with nothing good in them. While ministering to university students on campus, Christian ministers have to face different cultural barriers and practices that seem to contradict the Gospel. In such contexts, instead of overthrowing and rejecting the cultural barriers, the minister needs to find points of contacts to create better relationships with students of other faiths.

The second method is accepting everything that is in the local culture without questioning, which is called "Uncritical contextualization." The danger is that "if Christians continue in beliefs and practices that stand in opposition to the Gospel, these in time will mix with their newfound faith and produce various forms of neopaganism."[33] This kind of approach leads to radical syncretism which introduces unbiblical cultural practices into the fellowship.

The third method is called "critical contextualization," which evaluates the cultural and religious practices critically and adopts those that get along with Biblical values. In the process of critical contextualization, Hiebert recommends three steps. First, the missionary does an "exegesis of the Culture." The culture of other faiths needs to be studied thoroughly before passing any judgment. Secondly, he tries to interpret biblical truth in the light of other cultures and, thirdly, people of other faiths who are new believers should be given freedom to evaluate their cultural differences in the light of God's word.[34]

Critical contextualization leads to a holistic mission because it evaluates the culture and customs critically in the light of God's word. In this context, Dasan argues that "Critical contextualization neither denies the people's old cultural practices nor accepts them uncritically; rather it deals with the old by studying and critically evaluating it in the light of Biblical norms."[35] Critical contextualization avoids syncretism and dominance of other cultures. It helps to develop self-theology from within the context in the light of objective Biblical values.

These three models can be seen in the theory and practice of Christian missions among different faiths. Ministering to Muslim students in Indian universities is one of the greatest challenges in Indian missions. In this context, different contextual approaches that were proposed and developed by mission practitioners are relevant to people of other faiths, especially to unreached Muslim students.

2.3 Ministry among Muslims

In this section, different types of contextual models and mission practices among Muslims are discussed to adopt them for ministry to Muslim students. India has some of the best universities open exclusively to Muslim students such as the Jamia Millia Islamia University in Delhi, The Jamia Markazu University near Calicut and the Aligarh Muslim University in UP. "A survey conducted by the Aligarh Muslim University (AMU) shows that there are 92 modern colleges run by Muslims in various parts of India. Some of these colleges are similar to universities, taking into account the numbers of students and courses offered."[36] Almost all of these Muslim universities and colleges are untouched and the Christian presence is nil. The contextual ministry approach may help to establish a Christian presence on these campuses.

2.3.1 Different Approaches to Witness to Muslims

In his article "Approaches to the evangelization of Muslims" in EMQ (April, 1996), John Mark Terry suggests five models: confrontational, traditional evangelical, institutional, dialogical and contextual. These approaches can be found in ministry to Hindus as well but, in this section, we look at them in the context of ministry to Muslims. These approaches can be some help to witness among Muslim students on the campuses.

2.3.1.1 Confrontational Method

Some of the early missionaries, such as Henry Martyn, Karl Pfander and St. Clair Tidall used the confrontational method. According to my observation, there is no particular campus ministry that focuses exclusively on reaching Muslim students. This approach may not work these days because "today's missionaries prefer to emphasize the positive nature of the Gospel, rather than expose objectionable elements in Islam."[37] This confrontational mission method confuses people of other faiths and it may build bridges instead of clarifying the truth. Especially, "the way Christians interpret and use the titles of Jesus among Muslims are not only confusing but sometimes downright repulsive, leading many of them to reject the Word of God before they have a chance to consider its message."[38] The confrontational approach always uses rational apologetic tools to argue for the exclusive truth claims of the Christian faith. Campus ministries in India such as UESI, ICCI, and ICPF apply this apologetic method to reach Muslims which may not be welcomed by Muslim students.

2.3.1.2 Traditional Evangelical Method

Samuel Zwemer, who was called the apostle to the Muslims, used this method. He strongly argues for "church based" mission to Muslims. His theory is that the church as a body of Christ should take up evangelizing Muslims. He extensively travelled to many Muslim countries and challenged the church to take up the responsibility to witness to Muslim nations. In fact, he was the editor of *The Muslim World* for 36 years. According to Lyle Vander Warf's evaluation, Zwemer's approach is that "evangelism must deal with the incarnation, atonement and mediation in an experiential fashion."[39] This method also emphasizes a traditional type of apologetics and arguments for the exclusiveness of the Christian faith. This traditional evangelical approach is a type of western approach which practiced mission from the Western cultural perspective by neglecting the culture of the people. University students belonging to a Muslim background may not be interested in this church-based approach. They need an approach that is relevant to post-modern Islamic thinking.

2.3.1.3 Institutional Approach

In this approach, mission is practiced as institutional service to the society through different activities like education, medical service and social service. The theory behind this approach is that "the denominations of love, compassion, and humility will break down the walls of prejudice."[40] In order to win the confidence of Muslim students, this theory provides education and medical services to the needy. Most Christian workers adopt community developmental programs in their approach to relate with Muslims because "this practical dimension of help is appreciated."[41] Service to society is considered a preparation for the proclamation of the Gospel.

The significant aspect of this theory is that educational institutes prepare a way for Muslims to read the scriptures. The belief is that higher education would "overthrow the native religions and transform culture."[42] Because of this conviction, mission was practiced as promoting educational and medical facilities. Several mission agencies use this mission practice among the Muslims in general, but efforts to reach students of this community are few.

2.3.1.4 Dialogical Approach

This approach is much emphasized and used in outreach to people of other faiths in recent days, especially among Muslims. Campus ministries can adopt this approach to influence Muslim students. It is not only preaching to others, but also listening to other faiths that is important. The theory is that listening to other faiths will help the missionary understand others in a better way. In this mission practice, "the missionary does not surrender his convictions. Rather, he affirms them in a way that permits him to grow in his understanding of Muslims."[43] While emphasizing the dialogical approach to witness among other faiths, the WCC affirms the urgency of the proclamation of the Gospel. "The proclamation of the Gospel to the whole world remains an urgent obligation for all Christians and it should be carried out in the spirit of our Lord, not in a crusading and aggressive spirit."[44] This mission practice is present among ecumenical circles. Since university students give priority to thinking, this dialogical approach may yield some results. Campus ministers should learn to listen to Muslim students; then only they can relate with them. This approach motivates Christian workers to listen to Muslims, which is the need of the hour.

2.3.1.5 Contextual Approach

Students belonging to the Islamic background are untouched in India. Contextualized methods will be appropriate and, moreover, in outreach to Muslim students, "Contextual approaches are more likely to be effective among Muslims who are content with Islam, or who face considerable social pressure, than with Muslims disillusioned with Islam."[45] Christian missionaries committed to making an impact on Muslims developed this contextual approach. John Travis, a committed missionary who worked among Muslims for a long period in Asia, developed six contextual models in his theory and practice of mission to Muslims. John Stringer comments that Travis' contextual methods are "widely recognized and used as a benchmark of contextualization by Evangelical missionaries in the Muslim World."[46] His contextual models can be seen not only in the field of mission to Muslims, but also in Christian ministry to different cultures and religions. In this section, these models are discussed only in the context of ministry to Muslims. Even though these models are developed in a general sense to minister to Muslims, they can be a great help and relevant to ministry to Muslim students.

2.3.1.5.1 C_1 Model: Purely Non-contextualization

Western-type churches that existed in different local cultures have been using non-indigenous language in their worship and mission approach among Muslims in different countries. They isolate themselves from the local culture and, in fact, these Christian groups "exist as an ethnic/religious minority."[47] In some of the Islamic countries of the Middle East, the Orthodox Church has been practicing its ministry to Muslims in this C_1 model. For instance, "many English-speaking churches in former British colonies are good examples of the prior, while most Coptic churches of Egypt are good examples of the latter."[48] This model is not effective in witness because local people will not be attracted to the Gospel unless their local language is respected and accepted by the missionaries.

In some of the university and college campuses in India, Christian groups can be found which are not making much effect on Muslim students due to the non-contextualized mission approach. These types of Christian groups maintain their distinctive identity and they neglect local languages and cultural aspects. Muslim students are not attracted to the Gospel because there is no history of Arabic or Urdu Bible studies, seminars and teaching programs for university students in India. Christian organizations and churches invite Muslims and force them to listen to English messages and Christian theological jargon. In this context of communicating Gospel to the young people, Ron Hutchcraft says, "It may not be Christ they reject; it may be our religious vocabulary."[49] This model will not help the church to be an effective witness to Muslim students because language plays a vital role in receptivity to the Gospel.

2.3.1.5.2 C_2 Model: Indigenous Language and Christian Culture

In this model, indigenous language (Arabic and Urdu) is used, but Islamic culture is neglected. Only language is adopted but the terminology and the cultural practices are still Christian. Some of the traditional mainline churches established by western missionaries use the local language but the style of worship, liturgy, literature, musical instruments, etc., are still imported from western culture. Because of this mission practice, their presence among the Muslim community in India and elsewhere did not bring much results. Muslim students will be comfortable if we communicate the Gospel in their cultural forms that are permitted by the Bible. Thus, this C_2 model of contextualization may not be relevant and effective in ministry to Muslim students.

2.3.1.5.3 C_3 Model: Contextualization of the Culture

This model suggests the adoption of "insider cultural forms." Most Muslim-background believers are found in this type of model. They gather in church buildings as well as in unbiased places for worship to be more relevant to the culture of the new believers. "The aim is to reduce the foreignness of the Gospel and the church by contextualizing to biblically permissible cultural forms."[50] It is a good attempt to be relevant with the new cultures, especially to Muslims. This model is sensitive to indigenous beliefs and practices. In this model the new believers will not be forced to adopt Christian cultural practices either directly or indirectly. The mission practitioners of this model allow the new believers to grow in a particular cultural context instead of imposing the missionaries' culture on them. University students belonging to Muslim background may be comfortable with this type of approach.

2.3.1.5.4 C_4 Model: Balanced Contextualization

This model gives priority to the identity of the Muslim community. In this model, only Muslim-background believers gather together for worship. They do not identify themselves as Christians, but are identified as followers of Isa. The theory behind this model is that the followers of Christ should remain within the community yet they should witness to Christ through contextual approaches by using insider language and cultural forms. Parshall strongly recommends the C_4 model in Muslim outreach. In his mission practice, he encountered severe opposition in Asia but he succeeded in witnessing to Muslim communities in spite of struggles. In one of the countries (which he kept secret), while he was ministering to Muslims, he was advised to change his C_4 model and, in fact, he was threatened with death. However, he continued his work and made an impact on that country with the Gospel of Christ.[51] This model will be effective in ministering to Muslim students and they may also respond quickly.

2.3.1.5.5 C_5 Model: Insider View

The fifth model goes a little further—it gives more priority to Islamic culture and neglects the exclusiveness of the Biblical teaching on cultural issues. This model raises many questions regarding the limitations of contextualizing the Gospel and mission practice. The followers of Christ remain within the Muslim Community and they remain as Muslims sociologically. They do not come under church-centric Christianity; instead, they establish "Messianic Mosques" for worship. "Some missiologists propagate the idea that instead of getting Muslims into the Church, Jesus should be brought into the Mosque. That would allow Muslims who decide to become followers of Jesus Christ to stay within the fold of Islam, just as Messianic Jews have stayed within Judaism."[52] This is a radical syncretism which may bring problems in new believers' lives. Initially, it may attract people to listen to the goodness of Biblical faith, but it also brings some of the unbiblical cultural beliefs and practices into Christian faith.

John Travis, in his mission practice, strongly recommends the C_5 model. He worked for decades among Muslims in Asia and he practiced the C_5 model in his mission work. Some scholars, such as Richard Jameson and Nick Scalevich argue that first-century Jewish believers remained in their Jewish background while following a new faith in Christ. They continued to worship in the Jewish temple (Acts 2:46, Acts 3:1). In the same way, in the C_5 model, "Muslim believers, like early Jewish believers, are forming their own communities within Islam, and learning to love one another in small home fellowships as believers in Isa."[53] The fact is that "most Muslims have never met Muslims who 'follow Jesus,' so the curiosity that results from their identification often leads to open doors to share their faith in Christ."[54] Initially, people may be interested in this new faith, but there is danger in this mission practice.

Parshall comments on the C_5 model as "unethical and sub-Christian activity." Parshall offers a case study to support his argument. One of his team members entered a Muslim mosque by giving the impression that he wanted to worship there. He joined with the Muslims as they prayed in the mosque. After the worship, the Muslims came to know that he did not intend to follow Islam, but just pretended to do so and he was almost killed.[55] In this model, Muslim students may respond easily to the Gospel but their faith may not be rooted in Biblical values because the Bible does not permit some of their cultural practices.

2.3.1.5.6 C_6 Model: Secret Followers

This model suggests that believers from a Muslim background should be allowed to follow the Lord secretly and they should not be brought into the organized church. These groups are underground followers of Christ. They do not declare themselves as the followers of Christ but observe their faith secretly, remaining in their own religious culture. Since they do not declare themselves as followers of another faith, the Muslim community identifies them as Muslims and they do not have any problem. These people are churchless Christians and this phenomenon is growing not only among Muslims but also in most other faiths.[56]

In the context of ministry among Muslim students, it will be good to help them to follow Christ secretly in the initial stage of their Christian life; but they would not be able to keep this up indefinitely. Some of the major decisions involving marriage and other religious and cultural ceremonies would force them to reveal their identity. In such situations, students get confused and some may go back to their faith because they are not prepared to reveal their identity. This is why it is better to educate them to reveal their new identity in Christ slowly to their community and they should be prepared to face the challenges involved in following Christ.

2.3.2 Principles for Witnessing among Muslims

In his approach to planting churches among Muslims, Dan Brown developed seven principles that may be helpful to apply when reaching out to Muslim students. He believes that planting churches among Muslims is possible through the systematic practice of these principles. His approach is a team approach. The first principle is Launching the Team, in which the team will be equipped with plans and strategies of church planting. In implementing the second principle, Preparing to Sow, the team gets intensively involved in learning the language and adjusting to Islamic culture.

The third principle is "Sowing." By this time, the missionary will be able to communicate the Gospel in the local language and in the light of local cultural values. The Gospel will be shared in a gentle manner, with sympathy, rather than in an aggressive and argumentative manner. In practicing the fourth principle, the missionary concentrates on making a disciple of the Muslim-background believer in order to train him/her as a leader to be useful for Christ. The church begins with the implementation of the fifth principle. Muslim-background believers will gather to read the scriptures and for fellowship. Local leaders will be trained in the sixth stage and the church will function on indigenous principles in the seventh stage.[57] These principles have been practiced by various missionaries in their approach to Muslims. Muslim students in India can be reached through the implementation of these principles.

2.3.3 Sensitive Issues in Ministry among Muslims

There are some sensitive issues that we need to keep in mind when we engage in ministry to Muslims. The first issue is dealing with the culture. Cultural issues hinder Muslim students from accepting the Gospel. In this context, Travis argues that resistance to the Gospel from Muslims is not theological but cultural. He further suggests that "for the sake of God's kingdom much of our Missiological energy should be devoted to seeking a path whereby Muslims can remain Muslims, yet live as true followers of the Lord Jesus."[58] Muslim students who accept the Christian faith should not be forced immediately to come out of their cultural background and face issues which are very sensitive.

Baptism is the second issue that should be addressed in a sensitive manner. The Muslim-background student who follows Christ should not be forced to immediately take baptism because it is a great threat to their faith. In this context, the missionary needs to adopt innovative approaches to avoid misconceptions on conversion. In the context of ministry to Muslims, Parshall suggests "Self Baptism". He recalls an incident which could be an example to follow. He narrates that one of the seekers in a Muslim country was convinced that he must take water Baptism. Instead of going through with a traditional type of baptism, he himself went to a river and pronounced "'I now baptize myself in response to the command of Jesus Christ', and submerged himself completely under the water. Within a few weeks, this believer went on to baptize two other new believers from that area. The missionaries have accepted this baptism as legitimate."[59] Such approaches and practices avoid unnecessary confusion on conversion.

The third issue is the place of Muslim-background believers in the organized church. Muslim-background believers were not much welcome in the organized church. In fact, "there is the perennial doubt about the sincerity of Muslim converts."[60] In this context, Parshall developed a theory that gives priority in mobilizing the national church. His theory is that, through the national church, missionaries can relate with local Muslims in a better way. In his practice of mission among the Muslims in the Philippines, he organized consultation programs for national leaders through which he could challenge the native church to relate with Muslims.[61] The Muslim-background students who follow Christ often endure a lot of struggle due to the suspicious spirit of the church. Thus, Muslim-background students should be welcomed into the church without any hesitation.

2.4 Ministry among Hindus

Ministry to Hindu students in India is the greatest challenge and the need of the hour because "80% of the people are Hindus and the cultural atmosphere of the nation is definitely marked by the imprint of Hinduism."[62] In most of the Indian Universities "Sangh Parivar" activities are attracting these Hindu students, which is a challenge to minister to them. The church has failed, in a sense, to relate to these Hindu students so as to be an effective witness in the campuses. There are a few organizations that are working among universities and colleges in India but their impact on Hindu students is minimal compared to the population of Hindu students in the country. The appropriate methods and scholarly literature related to mission among Hindu students is not available to give relevant training to the youth workers. The traditional mission methods, models and theories which are used in ministering to Hindus in a general sense are used in mission to Hindu students in most of the youth organizations. Thus, I have taken such mission methods and theories to review the literature, in this section, to derive principles for an effective mission among Hindu students.

H. L. Richard rightly evaluated evangelical approaches to mission among Hindus in his research article, "Evangelical Approaches to Hindus"; here he summarizes five approaches which are thoroughly discussed along with some other theories. These approaches also can be applied to other faiths but here we look at these approaches in the context of ministry to Hindus. These approaches can be some help in mission to the students of Hindu faith. Some of these approaches may be found in the campus ministries in Indian campuses.

2.4.1 The Simple Gospel Approach

The traditional evangelists argue that man-made strategies and theories are not necessary to evangelize Hindus. The simple Gospel has the power to transform any religious community which is why we should not depend on any strategy. Richard calls it "non-approach" and he further comments that "non-approach 'simple Gospel' practitioners are in fact preaching a Western Gospel rather than a relevant message that reverberates in the local context."[63] In order to be relevant to the Indian Hindu cultural context, the Gospel must be presented in the context of the people of India.

2.4.2 Pentecostal Power & Pragmatic Approaches

Pentecostal or charismatic churches have made a great impact on the evangelization of India. These charismatic churches have penetrated into the hardcore Hindu localities. The truth is that "Indians are more power conscious than truth conscious in their religious beliefs."[64] Because of this reason Pentecostals are welcomed into Hindu societies and their impact is noteworthy. In the context of students' ministry in India, some of the organizations such as Assemblies of God (AG), Blessing Youth Mission (BYM), Inter Collegiate Prayer Fellowship (ICPF), Youth With A Mission (YWAM), etc., are working among the students. Most of the Pentecostal churches, especially Assemblies of God (AG) churches, have been attracting students from Hindu backgrounds. In fact "contemporary India is an India struggling against terrible odds, facing the almost unconquerable problems of population explosion, hunger, economic poverty, inequalities and injustices, in which hope is a vanishing commodity."[65] In this context, the pragmatic approach that is practiced by most of the Pentecostal ministers offer hope to the needy. Indian students may get attracted to this approach.

2.4.3 Fulfillment Theory

J. N. Farquhar was the main individual who developed the fulfillment theory which promotes "Christ as "the fulfillment of Hinduism." According to Farquhar's theory Christ was predicted in Hindu scriptures and these Hindu scriptures should be used as tools to proclaim the uniqueness of Christ whom Hindu scriptures have predicted. When Farquhar reached India in 1891, missionaries' attitude to Hinduism was confrontational rather than sympathetic. He developed a sympathetic approach to Hinduism through his writings such as *Gita and Gospel* (1903), *A Primer of Hinduism* (1911), *The Crown of Hinduism* (1913), *Modern Religious Movements* (1914), *and An Outline of the Religious Literature of India* (1920).

In his analysis on Farquhar's legacy of mission work, Eric J. Sharpe comments that "what Farquhar was trying to say in *The Crown of Hinduism* was not always well understood, either by Hindus or by other Christians."[66] The main concept behind this fulfillment theory is that Christ is portrayed as Prajapati in Vedas and "he is also often briefly stated to be the sacrificial worship (yajña)."[67] The belief is that using Vedic scripture that supports the supreme sacrifice of Christ will get the attention of the Hindus. The weakness of this theory is that the Hindus may not be comfortable when Christians use a few lines here and there in their scriptures to support their argument and ignore the majority of their scriptures that oppose the Christian faith. Hindu students in the campuses are not much aware of their ancient scriptures and much influenced by Western cultural practices due to media. In this context going back to the ancient scriptures of Hindus may not be much help to influence Hindu students in the campuses on a large scale but certainly this approach may result in building a rapport to communicate the Gospel to the students.

2.4.4 World-view Confrontation

In this approach the Hindu monistic world-view is confronted by rational arguments. Nehemiah Goreh was an example of this approach. His approach was to "defend Christianity by rationally refuting Hinduism."[68] His approach was a rational and traditional Western type of confrontation. Traditional Hindus may not welcome this approach because they "sit lightly to intellectualizing" religious faith. The fallacies that we point out may not be fallacies for them because they hold on to a cyclical frame work which ignores historical, rational thinking. Since university students may give some attention to rational thinking this type of approach may certainly give some results in ministering to Hindu students in Indian campuses.

2.4.5 Inculturation Method

The Inculturation model takes the existing culture as a base for the communication of the Gospel "Etymologically, 'inculturation' means the insertion of new values into one's heritage and worldview"[69] and it is understood to be, "...the dynamic relation between the Christian message and diverse culture; an ongoing process of reciprocal and critical interpretation and assimilation between them."[70] This approach goes for a "radical contextualization of the Gospel" which tries to translate the Christian message into local cultures and "into indigenous religious forms" to be more effective.[71]

Since Hindus give high regard to the culture, this inculturation method is very much welcomed by them. Even though this mission method is developed to be relevant to the culture, Richard suggests that this method is essential and relevant to reach Hindus in India. Inculturation mission practice is very much present among Catholic circles in India. In fact it was the Catholic Church which popularized this mission method among Hindus in India. Samuel Rayan, one of the renowned Catholic theologians in India, argues that "it was through a process of linguistic, theological and liturgical inculturation that the New Testament sought to communicate a message."[72] The main purpose behind this theory is that "the Gospel is being given a new opportunity to penetrate the totality of Indian culture and thinking to become native and original."[73] The high-caste Hindus are very much attracted to the Catholic Christian faith in India because of their inculturation mission practice. For instance the Reddy community, one of the Hindu high-castes, in Andhra Pradesh, is very much influenced by the Catholic Church. Since, religious pluralism prevails in the Indian college campuses this method will attract the students from Hindu background but the dangerous thing in this method is that it leads to syncretism and minimizes the exclusiveness of the Gospel.

2.4.6 Homogenous Unit Principle

This approach is developed mainly to reach people groups belonging to different nations, cultures and religions. Even though there are different people groups within Hinduism, Hindus at large can be considered a people group. This principle advocates that "people like to become Christians without crossing racial, linguistic, or class barriers."[74] People find comfort in their own kind of group and "men can become Christians without the actual local experience of crossing racial or class barriers; but they deny Christ if they refuse to cross such barriers when crossing or not crossing them becomes an issue."[75] Hindus generally resist the Gospel due to issues of caste. If there is a particular church exclusively for a particular caste, people respond positively. Christianity in India is labeled as the religion of the Dalits and the high-caste Hindus think that Christ is a God of the Dalits. In this context, reaching high-caste Hindu students is a great challenge. Caste consciousness prevails in Indian university campuses. Even though there are disadvantages and a lot of criticism of the "Homogenous Unit Principle" it may help to some extent to impact different caste and class group students.

2.4.7 Contextual Approaches to Hindus

In the previous sections contextualization is discussed in a general sense and particularly in the context of ministry to Muslims but in this section some of the contextual approaches are discussed in the context of ministry to Hindus. Ebe Sunder Raj introduces a radical model of worshipping Christ in the Indian cultural context. He argues that Indian cultural practices should not be replaced by western Christian culture. He contextualizes some of the Indian cultural practices such as Tilak/ Pottu/Bindhi, ornaments, Arti, last rites of ancestors, respect for parents and teachers and festivals. His argument is that Sat Guru (Yesu) can be worshipped in the Indian cultural context without violating scriptural values.[76] In fact Tilak/Pottu/Bindhi are a mark of married women in Indian culture. In his mission practice he encourages these Indian cultural practices. He also contextualized some of the Hindu cultural practices such as Namakarnan and Pavitra Prasad (1 Cor: 11). He argues that "Lord's supper" should be introduced as Pavitra Prasad.

The fact is that "it is vital for any true approach that we try to get inside the mind of this new India and attain some real measure of self-identification with it."[77] The insider view of the Hindus should be considered in mission to the Hindus. There are several Indian Christian thinkers who developed contextual methods in order to relate with the Hindus which may prove useful to mission among Hindu students.

2.4.7.1 Hindu-Christian Identity

Some of the followers of Christ from a Hindu background in India identified themselves as "Hindu-Christians." The Hindu students who accept the Christian faith struggle for their identity due to various sociological and cultural issues. This theory may give them a new identity but it should be examined from the Biblical perspective.

Sattampillai, the founder of the Hindu-Christian Church of the Lord Jesus Christ, claimed that Hindu cultural practices are similar to Jewish cultural practices. He interpreted the term "Hindu" as geographical rather than religious and he understood Hindu customs as Indian customs.[78] This kind of "Hindu-Christian" identity is not seen in mission practice among Hindu students in the college campuses in India.

2.4.7.2 Churchless Christianity

The followers of Christ from a Hindu background in India are comfortable in Churchless Christianity because of traditional, cultural, social and political reasons. In fact, Christianity is growing in the Southern countries but this growth is happening rapidly outside the church. What I mean is that most of the followers of Christ from a Hindu background are not regular members of the traditional churches but rather their growth is taking place in different indigenous gatherings.

Dasan Jeyaraj illustrates this phenomenon of "churchless Christianity" in his research paper "Followers of Christ outside the Church and Missiological Education." One of the interesting findings from his research is that "in the data collected out of 12166 respondents, 390 declared to remain outside the Church. It is 3.20% as per the data collection." He further gives a caution by saying, "It is a huge movement and it cannot be ignored."[79] The Hindus in India wish to see the manifestation of the Gospel in followers of Christ because "the Hindus will not separate the preacher and the message, the evangelist and the Gospel, the truth and its manifestation."[80] The hypocrisy of the church becomes a stumbling block to the people of other faiths, as a result most of the Hindus remain in churchless Christianity and some of them do not want to identify themselves as Christians.

Hoefer in his research on churchless Christianity in Chennai found out that most of the Hindus and Muslims "remain outside the institutional church."[81] There may be many reasons for this, but the main reason is "community identity." In order to remain in their community some of the radical followers of Christ from Hindu background such as Subba Rao, Chenchaiah, Chekkraiah, Bramhobandha Upadhyaya, Narayan Vaman Tilak and Dayanand Bharati criticized the organized hierarchal concept of the church and suggested indigenous forms of expression. Yesu Darbar, a contemporary movement which is attracting Hindu folks in North India, founded by Rajendra B. Lal, is just an example to illustrate this phenomenon.[82]

The young people and the University Students are comfortable with this churchless Christianity but this is not a good trend to accept because "Churchless Christianity is clearly a departure from historic ecclesiology."[83] The young people should be drawn to the church which is essential to derive spiritual nourishment and discipline.

2.4.7.3 Contextualized Indian Bhakti Tradition

Hindus in India give priority to Bhakti (Devotion) rather than rationalistic theology. In this context, Sunder Raj suggests "the uniqueness of the Sat Guru must be communicated in public to our fellow Indians through the vehicle of Bhakti."[84] The tradition of Bhakti becomes a referring point to communicate the Gospel.

Subba Rao developed a contextualized Christian practice and his mission practice goes along with the Indian Bhakti tradition. "Subba Rao appeared more Hindu than Christian is a positive rather than negative point."[85] He openly rejected baptism and the organized church. He identified himself as a "Hindu Christian" and his mission practice uses more of the inculturation method.[86] Subba Rao's mission method falls under the "Uncritical contextualization" method which was explained by Hiebert. Hiebert explains this uncritical contextualization as a mission practice which accepts traditional practices in to the church without questioning the practice.[87] Subba Rao used the Bhakti tradition which is relevant in Indian context but crossed biblical boundaries in his mission practice.

Bakht Singh was another man of God whose contribution in mission to Sikhs and Hindus is noteworthy. Most of his church members are from non-Christian background. The secret of his success is practicing an Indian style of worship. His church is completely indigenous in look as well as in the worship pattern.[88] His methods are relevant to the Indian Bhakti tradition. He contextualized his methods to attract Indian Hindu crowds by using Indian musical instruments and an Indian style of worship. Devotion to God through reading of the scriptures and prayer is given supreme priority in his mission practice. He gave lot of importance to devotion in his mission practice which made him succeed among the Hindus.

The concept of discipling is prevalent in the Indian Hindu religious tradition. In fact, "the concept of discipleship is thoroughly Eastern and Indian. It holds a deep appeal to the Indian psyche. The Indian mind estimates the genuineness of a spiritual message by the degree to which it is practiced and therefore concretized."[89] Dayanand Bharati affirms this and he uses this discipleship method in his mission practice. He addresses Christ as "Sat Guru, term" which is familiar to an average Indian Hindu. "The practice of Christian discipleship in an Indian cultural form is both communicable and involves the whole church in the task of mission."[90] Hindu students in the college campuses need this type of discipling approach in order to mentor them spiritually.

2.5 Ministry to the Students in the Campuses

The practice of Christian Ministry to the students in the university campuses was mainly developed by Western ministries in their universities. Since most of the methods and mission practice among students are derived from the West the available literature is found in the international sources which can be applied to ministry among Indian University students. Christian mission work needs serious attention to impact students of different cultures, religions and backgrounds because it is the student community that plays a vital role in socio, political and economic issues of the society in almost all the countries. In fact "most of the students finalize their philosophy of life and their lifestyle while they are in college. Before entering college, students are influenced by parents and friends. During college, students are open to new ideas and influences."[91] It is not easy to minister to the students because they are time-conscious when it comes to religious activities.[92]

The history of missions is the history of student movements. In the midst of changes, challenges and struggles Christian ministry among university students steadily grew in the history of missions. Christian students in the campuses started forming different societies mainly from the early 1800s starting from Harvard and Yale Universities. Sabin P. Landry gives three reasons for the development of the societies related to student ministry. The first reason is theological students started meeting to discuss various ethical and theological issues which led to the formation of theological societies; the second reason is Christian students started meeting for prayer, Bible reading and fellowship which led to the formation of societies focused on the spiritual aspect; the third reason is students who are interested in "missionary enquiry" started forming societies that focus on missions.[93]

Throughout history several student movements such as Young Men's Christian Association, Young Women's Christian Association, Inter-Varsity Fellowship of Evangelical Unions and Student Christian Movement made a tremendous impact in university campuses in the area of social service and campus evangelism. The history of Christianity is mainly influenced by the student movement which played a major role in Christian mission. Mission to students in the university and college campuses is a thrust area that needs attention because "the future of the church is being fashioned in a microcosmic way on the college campus."[94] Thus, in order to strengthen the church in India, we need to focus effective mission to students of different faiths in Indian universities.

Ministering to students of different religious backgrounds in the college and university campuses is a great challenge because of the revolutionary changes and challenges in the present scenario. B. K. Tettey comments that "the students we meet on the campus are the products of a thoroughly secular society which in practice has rejected the claims of Christ and has succeeded in pushing the Church out of her social and intellectual life."[95] The Christian students who are influenced by the secular environment are also skeptical about Biblical faith. In this context the campus ministers "bring an agenda to the university not really offered anywhere else: addressing the spiritual side of the human community in ways that will contribute to the health of the entire university environment."[96] There are different models and methods tried and proposed to reach students of different faiths in the campuses.

2.5.1 Evangelism through Education

Most of the early missionaries became involved in establishing educational institutions hoping that they would "effect individual conversions" among the students.[97] Alexander Duff should be remembered in this theory that promotes mission to students through education. Duff visualized that Indian crowds can be evangelized by offering English education which may enlighten young people to think. Indian Mission history reveals that "the first college in Asia was founded by the British Baptist missionaries Carey, Marshman and Ward in 1818 on the outskirts of Calcutta."[98] St. Stephen's College in New Delhi, Madras Christian College, St. John's College in Agra, Christian Medical College (CMC) in Vellore and Ludhiana and Allahabad Agriculture University are just a few examples among numerous higher educational institutions established by the missionaries.

The original purpose of establishing these Christian institutions was to propagate the Christian faith but it "has never been fulfilled in the past and is now incapable of fulfillment."[99] Of course, there may be some efforts "but the efforts to win converts through these educational institutions have not been much of a success any time, and some sections of the Church in India and abroad see no sound basis for the continued existence of these colleges in as much as they are apostolically ineffective."[100] Certainly there may be an influence on students of different faiths through these educational institutions but the impact is very less.

2.5.2 Chaplaincy in the Christian College Campuses

Christian missionaries and mission agencies across the globe made a great impact on education by establishing colleges and universities. The Christian institutions can appoint a chaplain to take care of the spiritual needs of the students because "the amount of time campus ministers are actually involved with a given student is relatively brief compared with a pastor in a parish."[101] In the Indian context, Christian colleges lack this approach which is essential to cater for the spiritual needs of the students because "the university chaplain will be a person who will consider the whole community of students, academic and non-academic staff as his 'university parish.'"[102] He will become a bridge to create a spiritual environment in the campus because "Campus ministers are 'bridge-builders' among people of faith, people searching for faith, and all others in the academic environment."[103] This approach may not be applicable because most of the Christian colleges in India are undertaken by the Indian government and religious activities are not allowed officially by the administration of the college.

2.5.3 Interfaith Worship

Interfaith Worship centers in the university campuses are a recent phenomenon practiced by people who are influenced by pluralistic thinking. It will be welcomed and well-received in the context of a religiously pluralistic country like India. The purpose of interfaith worship centers is to create spirituality among students irrespective of their religious background. Students of different religious backgrounds come together to worship by holding their convictions and beliefs. Every one worships according to their convictions but they do it in a common place. This is one of the radical approaches to relate with people of other faiths while respecting their beliefs and convictions. The belief is that Christian students get a better chance to witness to students of other faiths through their way of conduct and faith.

"Kay Spiritual Life Center" at American University has this type of interfaith worship center in which different religious background students of the University worship together in harmony and its "campus ministry includes Buddhist, Catholic, Christian Scientist, Jewish, Muslim, Protestant, and Vedic/Hindu communities."[104] The members do not give up their convictions but rather they respect each other in a friendly atmosphere. Those who are attracted by other faith convictions can follow them but there will be no direct or indirect influence to convert the other.

This model of witness among campuses may not serve the purpose in Christian witness because Christian witness includes verbal proclamation regarding the uniqueness of Christ among other faiths. The exclusiveness of the Christian faith will be minimized because of this approach and at times Christian students need to take a stand against cultural and religious practices of other faiths. Thus, this approach may not be appropriate to witness to other faiths among Indian university students.

2.5.4 Hospitality

Hospitality is one of the requirements to reach students of different faiths in the campuses. Students migrate to different cities for education. These migrant students look for a homely atmosphere where they get love, acceptance and fellowship. International Students Ministry (ISM) which came in-to existence in the year 1996 in Illinois emphasizes giving "hospitality" to students in the campuses in their mission practice to relate with them.[105] This is one of the best methods to reach students at our door steps. It is not easy to reach Muslim students in some of the Middle Eastern Islamic Countries due to restrictions but many of them migrate to other countries for better educations. These students who are away from their home town and nation are open to the Gospel if we relate with them in a friendly manner. These students can be reached through hospitality because these "students need a safe place to ask critical questions, work through doubts to a deeper understanding of faith…" Thus, hospitality in open homes in the campus "offers a powerful milieu and a critical set of gifts in the formation of meaning, purpose, and faith."[106] Most of the mentoring opportunities for students come from giving hospitality to them.

Mentoring young people is the greatest need of the hour because "ongoing research makes it increasingly evident that those who are able to work on behalf of personal and social transformation are those who as young adults were a part of a mentoring community."[107] Serving good food to these young students is essential because there is a proverb which says, "The door to reach a young man is through the stomach." There is truth in it because students who stay away from their home miss homely food, thus we get a listening ear from the students if we offer food. Another advantage is that "conversations around food offer a welcoming and nourishing atmosphere for persons with different faith perspectives to be comfortable and authentic around one another."[108] Since, Eastern religions and cultures give high value to hospitality, it should be practiced in our mission approach to relate, mentor and impact the university students of different faiths in India.

2.5.5 Personal Evangelism

Personal Evangelism is one of the most effective methods to witness to people of different faiths. In this method the evangelist relates in a better way to understand the student's mind and his level of thinking. Most of the Hindus and Muslim students get attracted to the Gospel through personal evangelism. The sad thing is that "this form of evangelism suffers greatly from the too common idea that it is confined to the spoken word."[109] Personal evangelism is not just verbal proclamation but rather in this method the evangelist's life becomes a living witness to the students of other faiths. Students of other faiths, especially in a country like India, are sensitive to their beliefs and practices. In this context, our evangelism must be practiced in "humility and love and with due concern for the proprieties of time and place."[110] College campuses are filled with violence and insecurity, due to various socio, political and economic reasons. In this context, our witness brings healing and reconciliation through personal relationships.

2.5.6 Group Bible Studies and Discussions

Group Bible studies and discussions attract students of different faiths to participate in lively discussions that lead to truth. Most of the ministries that have been working among campuses have been using this approach. The reason is that in group discussion students get a chance to interact with the truth and they get an opportunity to express their views which leads to dialogue. In our present day context "rejection and misunderstanding by peers is a key problem" and because of this problem group discussions attract students to express themselves in which "sharing could take place."[111] Meaningful discussions on different contextual and existential struggles can be linked to Biblical truth and ultimately students can be exposed to the Biblical truth.

2.5.7 Coffee House

The strategy of "coffee house" is one of the creative mission strategies to reach students of different faiths in campuses. It is a hangout for students of different faiths to meet for fun and entertainment which becomes a base for relationships. "In many respects the "coffee house" stands in the same relationship to the campus ministry as the church social supper does to the parish church: it provides a place for fun and fellowship, for meeting and making friends."[112] Hasan al-Ghazali, a missionary among Muslim students, practiced "coffee house" as a strategy to reach students in his mission practice and he says that "coffee house" "is like the central circle of a spider's web where you build up contacts in a network into all segments of society."[113] He named his coffee house as "Magha" and attracted different segments of people. He influenced police, teachers, and students. He narrates that "after finding interested people we visit their homes and involve the family in the friendship."[114] In the context of Indian youth, Jacob

G. Isaac has been practicing this coffee house model in his ministry among Bangalore youth. He named it as "Kerygma Coffee House" which also arranges "Kerygma Coffee Talks" on different youth-related issues.[115] Jacob is an inspiration for many youth workers in India to adopt this coffee house method. This is one of the creative strategies to relate with students of different faiths in the campuses.

Summary and Conclusion

UESI came into existence in 1954 with evangelical convictions to cater for the spiritual needs of students belonging to different faiths in India. Professor Enoch, an active member in SCM, was the initiator of this movement and his contribution to the movement shaped its theological thinking and mission practice. The movement gave priority to the spiritual needs of the students and it made a great impact in reaching out to the students in multi-faith contexts of India. It is an indigenous student movement but the ministry practice and principles are derived from Western student movements. The available literature related to theory and practice of mission to other faiths is reviewed to study the impact of UESI on students of different faiths.

Some of the Western missionaries in the past failed to see the distinction between religion and culture; instead they viewed culture as a part of religion which made them approach other faiths negatively. Believers from other faiths were encouraged to change their cultural practices and Western culture was understood as superior to other cultures. This type of confrontational attitude neglected contextualized ministry to other faiths. Present-day mission practice among other faiths, especially to Hindus and Muslims, demands contextual approaches. Contextualization helps the missionary to relate with other faiths in a better way. Critical contextualization methods may be adopted in ministry to other faiths, because uncritical contextualization may lead to syncretism.

Different contextual models are developed by John Travis in his ministry to Muslims in Asia because communicating the Gospel to Muslims demands a contextual approach rather than the traditional evangelical confrontational approach. His six models are "C_1 to C_6 Cross-Cultural Church-Planting Spectrums." These models emphasize language, culture, worship pattern and the identity of a Muslim background believer. In the case of Ministry to Hindus, contextual models and theoretical frame-works were not developed by the mission practitioners compared to Ministry to the Muslims. Richard's evaluation on evangelical Christians approach to Hindus may give some insights for assessing effective ministry to the Hindu students in the campuses.

Campus ministry in India needs serious attention, especially in that reaching Hindu and Muslim students need contextual approaches that are relevant to them. Hospitality, personal evangelism, coffee house, Group Bible studies and discussions and Inter-faith worship are some useful approaches to relate with students in the campuses. These approaches may help in interpreting the data here also.

Contextual models, sensitive issues, practical guidelines and mission practices among people of other faiths, especially among Hindus and Muslims that were discussed in this chapter will provide a theoretical frame work to evaluate the ministry of UESI's impact on students of other faiths. The research questions will be answered.

Chapter Three

Analysis and Interpretation of Data

Introduction

This chapter focuses mainly on the presentation and analysis of the data collected from the members of UESI to investigate the answers for the Research Questions. The data collected from the field includes 45 interviews and 120 questionnaires from EU (Evangelical Union), EGF (Evangelical Graduates Fellowship), and fulltime Staff of UESI who are acquainted with the ministry of UESI in Hyderabad. The significance of the data is that it includes response from Christian, Hindu and a few Muslim background believers who are mature and most of them are key leaders in the movement. Some of the available UESI documents also support the findings that have come from the field data.

The collected information from questionnaires has been systematically tabulated and presented in a simple manner through tables and figures for better understanding of the readers, and the reliable and relevant statements from interviews have been taken to analyze the questionnaire more realistically. In order to avoid confusion, the readers, need to understand that RQ refers to Research Question which deals with main sections of the chapter and QQ refers to Questionnaire Question.

There are four Research Questions in this chapter and each RQ is answered by the help of several QQs and interviews. The data is analyzed in the light of review of literature while interpreting the tables and at the same time a brief summary and analysis is also given at the end of every RQ This chapter mainly deals with the facts and figures related to the ministry methods of UESI among the students of different faiths, the response of the students to the Gospel, the impact of UESI on students and suggested methods for better ministerial methods and practices among the students of different faiths.

3.1 Ministry methods of UESI

UESI has been using some significant methods to reach students of different faiths in Indian university campuses. Anil, an EU leader from OU, says, "Indeed, the UESI ministry is a blessing for the youth and it has been influencing students of different faiths like Christian, Hindu and Muslim background students."[116] Since the movement is evolved from the Western Student movement called SCM (Student Christian Movement), its methods seem to be traditional and confrontational but very effective among Hindu students and nominal Christians compared to the Muslim students. On this issue Research Question 1 is designed to investigate the ministerial methods of UESI.

RQ1. What are the methods UESI employs in Hyderabad Universities in its Ministry among Christian, Hindu and Muslim Students?

Christian mission to the college students in the campuses is a hard task because, although it may not be difficult to start Christian witness in the campuses yet "it's very difficult sustain the ministry, because a student cannot stay more than three years. He finishes his course and relocates to other place by the time we try to train him after he accepts the Lord."[117] In the midst of challenges like this, the UESI ministry in Hyderabad is deeply rooted in the campuses and it has been impacting students from different faiths. The following ministerial methods are observed from the data collected from QQs and interviews. There are only three questions that are designed to answer this RQ, which is why all the answers of QQ 6 are discussed thoroughly with the help of information from interviews.

QQ 6: What is the most Effective Evangelistic ativity your cell is involved in?

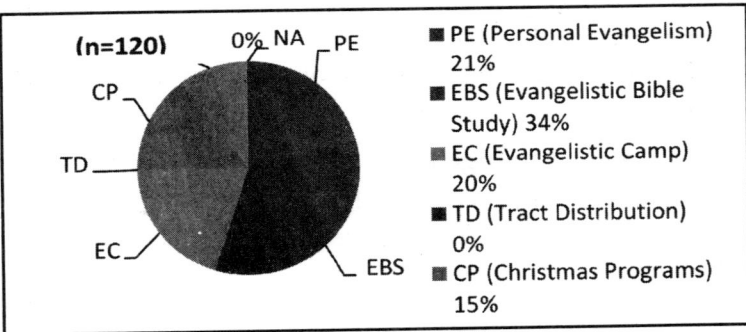

Figure 1: Effective Evangelistic Activities

3.1.1 Effective Evangelistic activities

Even though the above QQ 6 forces the respondents to tick only one answer, a few ticked more than one. As a result, 134 answers came from 120 respondents.

3.1.1.1 Evangelistic Bible Study

It seems UESI's most effective evangelistic activities are Evangelistic Bible Studies, Personal Evangelism and Evangelistic Camps. The majority of the respondents gave priority to these three methods which is evident from the above diagram. Out of the several methods that are mentioned in the diagram "Evangelistic Bible Study" is given priority because 34% responded to it. Group Bible Study is one of the effective methods of UESI in which "students' attention is drawn into the passage because of the questions that are raised. And the students are forced to observe the passage, understand the meaning and find some way to apply the meaning to their own life."[118] This is also called "Inductive Bible Study Method" which is effective among university students. That is why "whether at local level or district level, the students are coming to the Lord because of the Bible Studies."[119] The significant feature in these Bible Studies is that "students are the facilitators of the participatory discussion groups."[120] In my interview with people, a few responded that UESI uses a non threatening approach. Initially, they raise discussions such as "existence of God and the characteristics of God."[121] Thus, the students "move towards the personal relationship with the Lord because, a clear understanding of God, sin and salvation would be presented very clearly in the Bible Study."[122] The data clearly indicates that this Bible study method is effective among students especially in UESI ministry.

3.1.1.2 Personal Evangelism

Personal evangelism is one of the hallmarks of UESI's evangelistic methods. Twenty one percent of the respondents, which is the second largest opinion from Figure 1, expressed that Personal Evangelism is the most effective evangelistic activity of their cell. UESI encourages its members to practice Personal Evangelism as a day to day activity in their encounter with students. Anil confesses, "Personal Evangelism is the main method and this is the cutting edge for our ministry."[123] The members get special training in this area by having teaching sessions on it in almost all the discipleship and leadership level camps.

Now-a-days many people have raised hue and cry in UESI for having neglected this most effective tool. Traditionally UESI members engage in "meeting students individually and sharing personal testimony in a personal level, then inviting interested people to the small group inductive Bible Study."[124] It is distressing to note that nowadays personal evangelism is given less priority and it is neglected very much. Vikram reports, "In spite of all discussions and deliberations Personal Evangelism is drastically falling down."[125] On this issue M. Sudhakar comments, "I observe in our UESI circles a trend of replacing personal evangelism with program evangelism."[126] People become so busy with programs while neglecting personal evangelism, which is the most simple but fruitful approach. In the recent UESI's Annual General body meeting, "the floor expressed that the reason for lesser personal evangelism is mainly due to lack of role models who have zeal and enthusiasm for evangelism."[127]

3.1.1.3 Evangelistic Camps

Twenty percent of the respondents suggested evangelistic camps as being effective. The data shows Personal Evangelism and Camp Evangelism are equal with one percentage of difference to these suggested methods. Coming to the effectiveness of the camps, Subash, an EGF member, says, "In these evangelistic camps some of the practical talks and personal testimonies inspire the students."[128] Sudheer Prem Kumar looks at this approach in a realistic sense and comments, "Today students are busy, they can't spare two or three days in the camps. Even if they come they try to leave the camp in the middle. So we need to change our strategy."[129]

3.1.1.4 Christmas Programs

Fifteen percent of respondents suggested Christmas programs as an effective method to reach students of different faiths. Dayakar says, "Christmas is an occasion which we use to share about the Lord Jesus Christ to our friends. We conduct Christmas programs with a good speaker who can explain the significance of Christ's coming into this world."[130] UESI ministry in Andhra Pradesh has been practicing the tradition of organizing "Christmas programs" for the non- Christian students in college and university campuses. Some of the unreached colleges were reached by using this Christmas festival occasion. For instance, "Students witness was started in Agricultural University through Christmas meetings by getting permission from the registrar."[131] Usually, the believing students organize creative pre-evangelistic Gospel meetings in every city starting from the first week of November till the Christmas day. In fact, every year "about 30 to 40 Christmas programs are conducted in different places in the City of Hyderabad exclusively for students. Through those programs, lots of Non-Christians are coming to the Lord."[132] This may be an effective method to reach students of other faiths by using Christmas festival as an occasion to present the Gospel.

3.1.1.5 Tract Distribution

The significant observation in the data is that not a single person out of 120 suggested Tract Distribution as the most effective evangelistic activity. This response gives an impression that UESI's priority to tract distribution is less compared to other activities that are mentioned above. This is confirmed in my interview with Chandra Shaker who frankly admitted, "Giving tracts is one of the methods followed by UESI but we give less preference."[133] There may be several reasons in giving less priority for this method. In fact, "tracts might be better used for mass distribution as in street preaching, but tracts might not appeal to the more educated."[134] Usually, the student crowd need personal explanation and their doubts should be clarified to accept Christ. This may be one of the reasons that the movement may not be giving priority to this method.

3.1.1.6 Students Witnessing to Students

UESI "is student initiative ministry and students were given much preference to think and act in the ministry."[135] In this movement "a student will take care of his fellow students. He himself shares the Gospel with his friends. He will take them to Bible studies and he will pray for them and he is the one who is going to involve much more."[136] The most effective strategy in its evangelistic methodology is "Student witnessing to student" because "it's easy for a student to identify himself with another student to counsel and to witness Christ."[137] Ezekiel gives a reason for the students' active participation in the ministry, saying that "we are also imparting the uniqueness of the ministry of students reaching the students."[138]

3.1.2 Relevance of the Methods

SA-Strongly Agreed, AG-Agree, US-Unsure, DA-Disagree, SD-Strongly Disagree, NA-Not Answered

Table 4: Methods

QQ	(n=120)	SA	AG	US	DA	SD	NA
7	UESI is having Appropriate Methods	27%	52%	12%	6%	1%	2%
8	UESI is having same methods for all faiths	12%	51%	14%	18%	1%	4%

Analysis and Interpretation of Data 49

The interesting observation from the above table is that 27% of the respondents "Strongly Agreed" and 52% "Agreed" that UESI is having appropriate methods. This indicates that 79% of the respondents were convinced that UESI uses appropriate methods. At the same time 63% (12+51) agreed that they have same methods to reach the students of all faiths. Thus, this response may give an impression to the reader that the majority of the UESI members believe that they have similar methods to reach students of different faiths, which are appropriate to reach the students that belong to different faiths. This impression is confirmed while interviewing Dayanand, Hyderabad District coordinator of UESI. I asked him whether there are "relevant, creative and appropriate" programs to address students of different faiths. And he firmly replied, "Apart from Christmas programs there are no specific programs."[139] What he meant was that there are no separate programs to reach the students of other faiths apart from Christmas programs. Muntaj a Muslim background student in UESI has also confessed, "According to my knowledge there are no special programs or special efforts to reach Muslim students in UESI and I have not seen any one with a burden to share the Gospel to them nor distributing tracts."[140] This may be one of the reasons that its impact on the students of Islamic background is very poor. Thus, what we can understand from the data is that the members of UESI observe that UESI is using same methods to reach the students of all faiths.

The above conclusion, it is appropriate to use the same methods to reach the students of all faiths, can be suspected also because the 14% were unsure and 18% disagreed that UESI has similar methods for the students of all faiths. It suggests that there may be a chance that UESI uses different programs to different faith background students but it is not so clear from the data.

Summary and Analysis

The ministry of UESI has been a great blessing to the students in the Indian campuses. The outcome from RQ1 revealed that UESI has been using traditional evangelistic methods such as Evangelistic Bible Studies, Camps, Personal Evangelism and Christmas programs and these methods are still effective and bringing good results in the ministry. The significant observation from RQ1 is that "Student witnessing to student" is the major secret behind the effectiveness of these methods. Another interesting observation in this RQ1 is that UESI may not be having separate programs to different faith background students, instead the same programs for all faith background students. This might be one of the reasons for its ineffectiveness towards Muslim background students.

The movement's approach to the students that belong to other faiths is not negative in the way that some of the western missionaries looked at other religions in the history of missions but it uses a non threatening approach. At the same time there are no contextual methods apart from the traditional methods to reach students of other faiths.

The precedent literature suggested Personal Evangelism and Bible studies as effective methods to reach students of other faiths. William Carey gave priority for Personal Evangelism to impact high caste Hindus in his times. Joe L. Coker recalls Carey's method of evangelism and says that he was "deeply influenced by the model of the eighteenth-century Evangelical Revival in England, which emphasized preaching and personal evangelism above all else."[141] Even though Carey was known as a linguist, he was passionate for evangelizing the Brahmins of his times. He used to join with the Brahmins, who sit in groups at temples, and he used to raise the religious discussions through which he introduced Bible as "Christian Shasta."[142] He maintained good relationships with Brahmins and influenced them with personal evangelism. The Bible narrates such success stories of Personal Evangelism. Philip succeeded in baptizing an Ethiopian eunuch through this method (Acts 8:27); Paul used this tool in every place he visited. In fact, "As Paul demonstrated in all of his remarkable efforts in spreading the Gospel (Acts 13–28; cf. 2 Cor. 11:23–28), he believed that doing personal evangelism and making conscious choices to obey God are also absolutely essential in fulfilling God's plan."[143] It is a known fact that the mission agencies these days are drifting away from Personal Evangelism to Program Evangelism and UESI is also falling into this trap because M. Sudhakar says, "I observe in our UESI circles a trend of replacing personal evangelism with program evangelism."[144] The church growth movement introduced lot of strategies and programs which diverted mission agencies from Personal Evangelism to Program Evangelism. The church growth strategists argue that "Personal Evangelism, as practiced and understood in the individualistic western world, will never produce a church planting movement among the communal people groups of India, or anywhere else for that matter."[145] This church growth concept made a lot of impact on Indian missions and the attention is given to mass evangelism by neglecting the personal evangelism, thinking that it may take long years to establish Christian witness. UESI-AP also may be in this danger of over emphasizing on growth oriented concept. It seems the movement is depending on programs and strategies by neglecting the most essential and effective tool "Personal Evangelism."

In the context of reaching high caste Hindus, Richard refers to J. Z. Hodge's presentation on Evangelism in Tambaram conference in one of his articles. Hodge suggests mainly three methods to reach Brahmins, "one was personal evangelism on the lines of the Banaras United City Mission. The second was through ashrams as a point of contact. The third was literature."[146] UESI gives priority to Personal Evangelism and a little bit emphasis on literature but there is no mission practice related to Ashram. Personal Evangelism can be an effective tool to reach Brahmin students in our Indian universities.

Evangelistic Bible Studies is one the effective methods which is still relevant among students. In fact, Inter Varsity Fellowship (IVF) has extensively promoted this concept of Bible study in its ministry among university students. "The strength of inductive Bible study is that it helps students discover the meaning of the text for them and not depend on teachers and preachers. Meanings arise from the text rather than being forced on to the text."[147] Another truth is that "when people only engage in the study of several books of the Bible or excerpts from it, they have a limited view of a few trees but cannot perceive the forest,"[148] but in this "Inductive Bible Study Method" students are helped to understand the Biblical truth in a simple manner.

The respondents felt that the methods of UESI are relevant even though there are no contextual approaches. If we analyze UESI's methods in the light of John Travis' "C1-C6 contextual models" UESI may be using C2 & C3 models which are still under the influence of Western type of mission practice. A few respondents suggested quoting scriptures of other faiths which are fulfilled in the Bible especially in outreach to the students of other faiths.

3.2 Response towards the Gospel from Students of different Faiths

Mission among students of different faiths is a great challenge because the response from them towards the Gospel message may not be the same because sociological stigmas, cultural practices and religious convictions play a vital role in students' response to the Gospel. RQ 2 is designed to find out the response of the students who belong to different faiths.

RQ 2: What is the response of the students from Christian, Hindu and Muslim faiths towards the Gospel?

There are mixed feelings and responses from the members of UESI to the above RQ. Vikram, one of the key leaders of UESI, says, "Most of the students are feeling a vacuum in their hearts and they are searching for the truth, so when we are going and communicate the Gospel in a proper way, definitely they are responding very well."[149] It is easy to get their attention in comparison to the adults, if we present the Gospel in a way that it meets their intellectual and rational mind. In fact, for the past fifteen years I preached a clear Biblical Gospel in a number of University and colleges campuses in Southern as well as Northern Indian states, but there was not a single incident when I was asked to step down or to stop my preaching; instead, once an English professor canceled his lecture and asked me to preach to his M.A. English literature students within his own class room during his allotted lecture time in Dehradun. Students are somewhat receptive to the Gospel, but this receptivity may differ according to their religious background.

3.2.1 Response from Students of other Faiths

QQ 10: Students from other faiths respond to the Gospel positively?

Analysis and Interpretation of Data

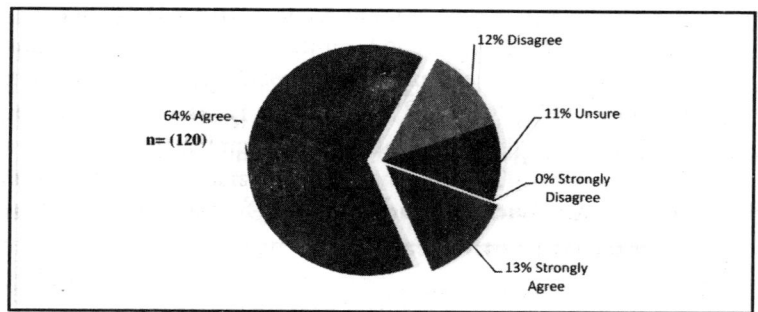

Figure 2: Response from other faiths

The word "other faiths" in the question refers to students who belong to Hindu and Muslim background. Even though an option is given, there is not a single person who has strongly disagreed that students from other faiths respond to the Gospel positively.

Seventy-seven percent (64+13) which is a huge percentage agreed that the students of other faiths respond to the Gospel positively. These "other faith" students may not be of higher caste groups from Hindu background. This fact is confirmed in my interview with Vikram, UESI-AP Executive committee Secretary who frankly admitted, "As for the statistics available with me, mostly we could reach students from SC (Scheduled Castes) background but not from higher castes. If we see the statistics, the majority of the students who are responding to the Gospel are SC background students."[150] The data informs us that forward Hindu caste groups are not responding much but mostly the good response is from SC background students.

When I enquired further, Vikram said, "seventy-five percent of the Hindu background students who are responding to the Gospel are from SC background students those who are already believing the Christian faith and who are going to church regularly; but they claim themselves as Hindus for the sake of reservations and the rest of 25 percent are from really Hindu background."[151] It seems there is lot of confusion in the response from the respondents. Seventy-seven percent of the respondents gave an impression that other faith students respond to the Gospel but according to Vikram's response we can understand that those Hindu background students who are responding to the Gospel are from SC background that are already exposed to Christianity. Thus, according to this data, students from high caste Hindus are not really responding to the Gospel but the majority of the response is from SC background students.

3.2.2 Christian background Students' response is high compared to other Faiths

QQ 11, 12 and 13 seem to contradict each other but the intention in designing these questions is to find out which religious background students mostly respond to the Gospel.

Table 5: Response from students of different faiths

QQ	(n=120)	SA	AG	US	DA	SD	NA
11	Mostly it is Christian background students who respond to the Gospel	22%	52%	10%	11%	3%	2%
12	Mostly it is Hindu background students who respond to the Gospel	16%	48%	12%	18%	1%	5%
13	Mostly it is Muslim background students who respond to the Gospel	0.5%	11%	27%	47%	10%	4.5%

The response for QQ 11 clearly affirms that the finding has come from the QQ 10 and the majority of the students who are responding to the Gospel are from Christian background students. The response from 74% (22+52) respondents for QQ 11 clearly affirms that those who responded to the Gospel mostly is from Christian background. This is the majority respondents' opinion in the above table. The reason for good response from the students of Christian background is that "they know the basics and they wait for somebody to talk and since they have Christian background and they

Analysis and Interpretation of Data

are in need of fellowship and friendship."[152] Dayakar agrees with John Paul in this fact and he says, "Nominal Christians are having primary knowledge about Christ when the truth is explained clearly, they are the one who are going to accept the truth immediately, but where as a Hindu sees the truth through different lenses. Thus, it is a little bit difficult for him to accept Christ."[153]

The Response from Hindu background students is also good because 64% (16+48) respondents informed that mostly it is Hindu background students who respond to the Gospel. Even though there is good response from Hindus, Bhimalingam suspects that this response might be from low caste Hindus. According to his understanding on this "high caste Hindus in Andhra Pradesh think that Christianity is the religion of the oppressed and low caste groups."[154] This might be one of the reasons that UESI's influence on Christian background students is high compared to other religions.

The response for QQ 13 is quite interesting. 57% (47+10) disagreed with the question which may help the reader understand that Muslim background students are not positive to the Gospel and they may not be receptive to it at all. This assumption is confirmed as fact in my interview with Muntaj, an EU student from Muslim background, who frankly admitted that "first of all they don't like to listen. They see any Muslim convert as a lost person who is destined to hell."[155] Another fact might be "Muslim students are a different kind of group because they never open to any kind of teaching except Islam."[156] There are practical instances to support this finding. For instance, "in Charminar Zone in Hyderabad, UESI conducted a Christmas program in 2007. There were a few Muslim background students who attended the program but they did not respond to the Gospel."[157] The majority expressed that they don't respond but at the same time QQ 13, informs us that a few respondents, 11.5% (0.5+11), agree that students from Muslim background respond to the Gospel. Thus, we can assume that the majority of the students from Muslim background may not respond to the Gospel but at the same time there may be a few students who respond to the Gospel positively.

Summary and Analysis

RQ2 investigated the response of the students from different faiths. The outcome for this question is that students from Hindu background are positive to the Gospel. In this context, Atul Y. Aghamkar comments, "There's tremendous interest among certain segments of urban Hindu society."[158] Especially, students who migrate to cities for education from other faiths respond to the Gospel. Aghamkar did a major study on this issue in the context of Pune and he found out that "Hindus of Pune to be more open to the Gospel than ever before."[159] This may be true in other cities as well.

Another conclusion from the data is that even though there is good response to the Gospel from Hindus, the new followers of Christ in the movement may not belong to forward caste groups. SC background students who are well acquainted with Christian faith but at the same time who are identified as Hindus in government records are the ones who are mostly responding to the Gospel. In fact Indian church is growing mainly among *dalits* and *tribals*. In this connection Frampton Frank Fox says, "Estimates suggest that 90% of Christians are from two segments of the Indian population: The Scheduled Castes and The Scheduled Tribes."[160] This may be one of the reasons that UESI's ministry is also mostly happening among the students with such background students.

The truth is that according to the Indian constitution, those who embrace the Christian faith from SC background have to forego some of the reservation facilities and they come under BC-C quota in all the government provisions because "the Constitution (Scheduled Castes) Order 1950, popularly known as the Presidential Order paragraph 3 says, "'No person who professes a religion different from Hinduism shall be deemed to be a member of Scheduled Caste.'"[161] To make it simple, "a Dalit who converts to Christianity loses his status as a member of the deprived classes."[162] May be because of this problem most of the SC background students who belong to Christian background identify themselves as Hindus in school and college records.

Another reason for the poor response from high caste Hindus and Muslims is that UESI is lacking contextual approaches to relate with them. Since the movement is evolved from the Western Student movements, its methods are effective among the students with

Analysis and Interpretation of Data 57

Christian background students. The traditional type of Bible studies may not attract the Orthodox Hindu students all the time. Caste is one of the major issues among the Hindus in India which may hinder them to respond to the Gospel. In this context, McGavran's observation, "people like to become Christians without crossing racial, linguistic or class barriers," is noteworthy.[163] UESI is not having any separate cells or fellowship groups on the basis of social order, which may be one of the reasons that high caste Hindu students are not responding much. There may be a reason from the movement's side to adopt such methods because UESI does not encourage such social and cultural distinctions on the basis of caste and class. In this context Hiebert's "Critical Contextualization" which was discussed in second chapter, the review of relevant literature can be a great help. In fact, "critical contextualization" approach evaluates the cultural and religious practices critically and adopts those who get along with Biblical values. It also avoids the danger of syncretism and makes the Gospel relevant to the students of other faiths.[164]

One of the reasons for non-receptivity towards the Gospel from high caste Hindus in India is that the "missionaries, whatever their country of origin, were viewed as agents of colonialism. The contempt that this misinterpretation engendered continues to be felt."[165] Even today, Christianity in India is viewed by high caste Hindus as a white man's religion and also "Hindus feel that Christianity is meant for Westerners and that Hindus should not be converted to it, for Christianity is a foreign religion."[166] In fact, "this disdainful attitude continues to be expressed toward Indian Christians."[167] This misconception is one of the great barriers for the receptivity of the Gospel. In this context, in order to win these high-caste Hindus, we need contextual approaches to win their confidence that Christianity is one of the Asian religions.

3.3 Mission among Students of different Faiths

This section is the major section that addresses the problem in a specific manner. There are 29 QQs that are designed to address RQ 3 which evaluates the ministry of UESI to Christian, Hindu and Muslim students. Apart from Table: 6, in all other tables three QQs which are related to three faiths (Christian, Hindu & Muslim) are clubbed together for better understanding of the impact of UESI to these faiths.

RQ 3: What is the impact of UESI on the students with Christian, Hindu & Muslim background?

3.3.1 Impact of UESI on Students of different Faiths

One significant impact of UESI on students in the campuses is the priority on transformation of the individuals. Students who come from different inferior backgrounds experience Christ like transformation by the efforts of UESI, because they help students to resemble Christ. Vikram Vardhan, one of the prominent UESI lay leaders, informs, "UESI is moving ahead in its impact on students because of its 'Core values' which are given priority in the movement."[168] In this context, Emmanuel, a Student leader from UESI, admits, "an egoist becomes humble, a person who is very proud becomes very simple and normal, a stingy person becomes generous. This ideal life style has really influenced Non-Christians."[169] During the past 55 years of its ministry UESI's impact on university campuses in India is significant, but which religious background students are influenced and who are the neglected is the major question. Its influence on students belonging to other faiths needs to be tested.

Table 6: Impact on students of three faiths
(Ch-Christian, H-Hindu, A-Atheist, O-Others, NA-Not Answered)

QQ	(n=120)	Ch	H	M	A	O	NA
1	What was your religious background	52%	45%	3%	0%	0%	0%
2	Majority students in UESI cell groups	51%	44%	0.5%	0%	2.5%	2%
3	Historically which religious background students are influenced by UESI?	42%	58%	0%	0%	0%	0%
4	Majority students in UESI leadership	58%	40.5%	0%	0%	0%	1.5%
5	Active Involvement of students background in UESI ministry	48%	51%	0%	0%	0%	1%

Analysis and Interpretation of Data 59

The above figure indicates that UESI's impact on students who belong to Christian and Hindu background is significant and it is almost at equal level. According to QQ 1, Christian background students are 7% higher than Hindu background students. This indicates us that Christian background members are more when compared to other faiths in UESI ministry. This fact is true according to QQ 2, and it is surprising to see that the Christian background students' majority in UESI cell groups is again 7% higher than Hindu background students.

Even though Christian background believers are the majority in UESI, the data indicates that UESI's impact on Hindu background students is significantly higher than Christian background students. The response for QQ 3 clearly affirms this truth. 58% of respondents indicate that Hindu background students were historically influenced by UESI, whereas only 42% of respondents show that the Christian background students were historically influenced by UESI. The influence of UESI on Hindu background students is 16% higher than Christian background students.

The response for QQ 5 clearly establishes the fact that Hindu background believers are actively involved in the ministry. This fact is confirmed in my interview with Daniel. Even though Daniel comes from a Christian background he frankly confessed, "Hindu background students' involvement is more compared to Christian background students."[170] In fact, "Those who understand the vision of UESI involve actively in the ministry. In this context, mostly Hindu background students are active in the ministry especially in Jawaharlal Nehru Technological University (JNTU), Hyderabad campus."[171]

It seems there is an apparent contradiction in the response from the people. The data clearly shows that the number of Christian background students are more in the movement (QQ 1), but at the same time the respondents informed us that it was Hindu background students who were also more historically influenced by the movement and they are ones who are actively involving in the ministry in UESI (QQ 3 & 5). Here the puzzle is, what is the reason for inactiveness of Christian background students in the movement and at the same time why UESI historically did not influenced Christian background students compared to Hindu background students?

I did not find any written documents on this issue and in fact this topic has not come in my interview with the people. Thus, I made phone calls to a few prominent leaders of the movement who can unfold the truth. B. V. L. R. Prasad, the Regional Coordinator of UESI for Hyderabad, explained, "It is true that the number of Christian background students are little bit more in the movement compared to Hindu background students, but their involvement in the ministry is less compared to Hindu background students." The reason he gave me is that "Hindu Students who come to the Lord are more passionate for the work of the Lord and they are more serious in following the Lord."[172] On this issue R. Srinivasa Rao, UESI full time staff for Hyderabad, said, "One of the reasons is that the Christian background students already have some kind of involvement in their local churches before they become members of UESI. Once they are in touch with UESI they have to involve in UESI as well as in the church, but in the case of Hindu background students they feel UESI as their whole and sole, which may be the reason that Hindu background students' involvement is more compared to Christian background students."[173] Vikram also informed me that "Christian background students are more in number in the movement but they are not really influential." The reason he gave me is that "Christian background students do not take Truth seriously because of their over familiarity." He further says, "Hindus students are growing in the movement qualitatively."[174] Thus, I conclude this issue on the basis of key leaders' information that the movement is growing quantitatively among Christians and growing up qualitatively among Hindus.

Coming to the question of leadership, it is Christian background students who are in the majority in taking leadership positions. QQ 4 informs us that Hindu background students' percentage in leadership is less compared to the Christian background students. Prasad explained, "According to UESI-AP's policy, leadership is given only to those who declare themselves as Christians in official records of the government."[175] There is a struggle for the SC background Hindu converts in the movements, if they declare themselves as

Analysis and Interpretation of Data 61

Christians in official records they have to forgo their reservation and they will not be considered as Scheduled Castes at the same time if they don't declare their faith they will not be given leadership responsibility in the movement.

According to my observation in the movement for the past 16 years, as a student leader and fulltime staff, most of the SC background students remain as Hindus in official records of the governments because of their struggle for existence, and as a result the followers of Christ from Hindus who belong to SC background will not get leadership opportunities in the movement. This is a well known fact in UESI circles. This is one of the serious issues the movement needs to think. The movement spiritualizes the political issue on faith declaration. *Dalits*, the SC background students have been oppressed by the elite sections of the country for centuries. Indian constitution also showed an injustice to them; because if a *dalit* converts into any other religion except Christianity he will continue to enjoy the privileges of reservation in government jobs and schemes but where as if a *dalit* converts into Christian faith he will lose his reservation status and all of the benefits. It is a struggle for existence and an identity crisis for the dalit Christian students.

The impact of UESI on Muslim background students is 0%. M. Sudhakar agrees with this and he says, "There is nothing very specially geared towards the Muslim students as far as my own knowledge goes back."[176] The State Secretary of UESI-AP, Sudhakar Rao, also stated that "apart from the rare incidents of students accepting the Lord from Muslim background, as a movement we could not influence Muslim student community."[177] This is true from the data because the interesting observation from the above table is that UESI's influence on Muslim background students is 0%. Even though several other options were given the respondents deliberately chose an answer, as the result the answer to the QQ 3, 4 & 5 is 0% under the column Muslim. It means Historical influence, developing students in leadership and active involvement of the students belong to Muslim background is 0%. There may be several reasons for the unfruitfulness of the ministry among Muslim students, but "to admit frankly the ministry among Muslims by UESI is very less."[178] One of the possible reasons is that the movement's approach to Muslim students may not be relevant.

Similarly in QQ 4 & 5 their presence in leadership and active participation in the ministry is 0%. In fact the movement's influence on Muslim background students is 0% according to the response from QQ 3. On the basis of these facts, we may assume that there may be some problems in giving personal care and effective follow-up for these 3% believers of Christ from Muslim background in the movement, otherwise why cannot these 3% students come up in leadership and active participation in the ministry? The movement may be neglecting spiritual nourishment for the believers of Christ from Muslim background. The other aspect is that the Muslim converts may not be comfortable in the movement or they may not showing genuine interest in new found faith. The problem can be from both sides, the movement as well as from Muslim background students. On this issue Muntaj frankly admits, "I cannot blame UESI alone for lack of ministry among Muslims and also I do not say that UESI is not doing anything to influence the Muslim students, but they are not coming up to that level."[179] Another significant observation is that "the percentage of Muslim background students' in Universities is proportionately very less."[180] The reason is that the percentage of Muslims in India is significantly less compared to Hindus and at the same time students who come up to university level education from Muslim background is again also very less. Thus, obviously the movement's impact on this group can be less but it should not be completely 0%.

3.3.2 Programs for Students of different Faiths

The percentage in the table refers to the number of respondents who ticked that particular column out of 120 total respondents. The questions in the table may not be very clear and appropriate to the respondents because some of the respondents did not get the right column to tick; that is why they have chosen open-ended column which I named as "Any Other." Those who mentioned the number of programs as four or more in the open ended space were placed under the column "More than thrice." The rest who wrote different things in open ended space were placed in the column "Any other."

Analysis and Interpretation of Data

This "Any Other" column is explained for the better understanding of the reader.

Table 7: Programs

1. Once, 2. Twice, 3. Thrice, 4. More than thrice, 5. Not at all, 6. Any Other, 7. Not Answered

QQ	(n=120)	1	2	3	4	5	6	7
21	No of programs for Christian background students in a year	10%	18%	24%	7%	26%	11%	4%
29	No of programs for Hindu background students in a year	14%	23%	21%	3%	24%	9%	6%
37	No of programs for Muslim background students in a year	5%	8%	3%	0%	66%	7%	11%

The intention behind asking these questions is to find out whether there are any special programs conducted exclusively on the basis of their religious background. It seems UESI conducts similar programs for all faith background students in its ministry. This assumption may be true from the careful observation of the above table under column 5 (Not at all). The majority of the respondents for QQ 21, 29 & 37 have answered the column "Not at all" which informs that UESI does not conduct programs especially for Christian, Hindu and Muslim students. Their intention in choosing this answer, "Not at all", might be a way of saying that UESI doesn't conduct programs on the basis of religious background but rather similar programs for all faith students. It has been confirmed this argument in interview with Muntaj, who frankly admitted that UESI conducts "same programs for all faith background students." She further says, "I have never seen any special program organized exclusively for Muslim background students."[181] Muntaj's statement seems to be a contradiction to the response for QQ 37, because the response to QQ 37 informs us that there are programs for Muslim students. What she might have intended is that there may be programs for Muslim background students but there are no programs exclusively for them.

A similar observation can be found in the response for QQ 21. QQ 21 indicates that 52% (10+18+24) of the respondents agreed that there are programs for Christian background students but Raju, a Christian background student, clearly mentioned, "No separate programs for Christian background students."[182]

A good number of 11% of the respondents have chosen open ended space "Any other" for QQ 21. Among these respondents Raju clearly mentioned that "No separate program for them."[183] A Muslim background believer, Rahmatulla, mentioned, "No specific programs are arranged."[184] There are some other comments such as "Not exclusively for Christians," "Programs are conducted for all," "General," "Programs for all," "For all." There are some others who mentioned "Weekly" "I don't know," "Unsure" "Quarterly one program." It is a clear indication from these respondents that UESI does not conduct separate programs for different faith background students but it conducts the same programs for all faith background students.

Under "Any other" column Divakar Reddy commented to QQ 29 that "no separate programs are conducted."[185] In the same way, for QQ 37, Sugunakar mentioned, "general for all not specifically for Muslims."[186] Thus, on the basis of these findings, we may come to the conclusion that UESI conducts programs for Christian, Hindu and Muslim students, but no programs are designed exclusively for students with different religious background.

3.3.3 New Believers in Every Year

QQ 19, 27 & 35 are a little bit complicated questions to interpret because they have two separate questions within one question. Since there are two separate answers for each question with different frequency, each question is divided into two separate questions as (a) & (b) to interpret meaningfully.

Analysis and Interpretation of Data

Table 8: New followers of Christ in percentages

QQ	(n=120)	Yes	No	Not answered
19 (a)	Are there any new believers added from Christian background to your EU cell?	85%	14%	1%
27 (a)	Are there any new believers added from Hindu background to your EU cell?	84%	9%	7%
35 (a)	Are there any new believers added from Muslim background to your EU cell?	22%	70%	8%

The word "added" in the questions above refers to the new followers of Christ those who have accepted the Lord recently and are attending the UESI fellowship meetings. QQ 19 (a) informs us that 85% of the respondents informed that new followers of Christ from Christian background students are added to the fellowship at the same time QQ 27 (a) informs that 84% of the respondents agreed that new followers of Christ from Hindu background students are added to the fellowship.

This data from table: 8 shows us that the new followers of Christ from Christian and Hindu students are adding to the fellowship in almost equal percentage. The important observation from the response for QQ 35 (a) is that 70% of the respondents confessed that there are no new followers of Christ from Muslim students in their cell. Thus, we can predict from the above table that there may be a good number of new followers of Christ from Christian and Hindu students but there may not be many followers of Christ from Muslim students.

Table 9: New followers of Christ in figures

1. Once, 2. Twice, 3. Thrice, 4. More than thrice, 5. Not at all, 6. Any Other, 7. Not Answered

QQ		a	b	c	d	e	d
19 (b)	If yes, how many Christian students added in this academic year (2008)? (n=102)	7	44	28	12	4	7
27 (b)	If yes, how many Hindu students added in this academic year (2008)? (n=112)	13	64	14	7	2	12
35 (b)	If yes, how many Muslim students added in this academic year (2008)? (n=27)	18	7	2	0	0	0

Coming to the particular number of new followers of Christ every year, 64 respondents for QQ 27 (b) informed that 2-5 Hindu students are accepting the Lord in their cell every year. In fact response to QQ 27 (b) is quite high compared to other two QQs 19 (b) & 35 (b) in the table (9). The 91 (13+64+14) respondents informed that Hindu students have added to the fellowship which is the big number in the table (9). This shows that, the percentage of new followers of Christ from Hindu students in every year in a particular cell is somewhat higher than, that of other faiths. If we go to the in-depth analysis the Hindu students who have been added to the fellowship may not be really Hindus. To put in the words of Vikram (Executive Secretary, UESI-AP) who frankly admitted that "seventy five percent of these Hindu students who are responding to the Gospel are from SC background students who already exposed to Christian faith and who go to church regularly but for the sake of reservations they claim themselves as Hindus and the rest of 25% are from really Hindu background."[187] Thus, we may understand that a good percentage of Hindu background students are adding to the fellowship every year, but many of these Hindus may be from SC background, who are already exposed to the Gospel.

Analysis and Interpretation of Data 67

The response for QQ 35 (b), 7 agreed that 6-10 Muslim students are accepting the Lord every year in their cell. This response shows that there may be a few new followers of Christ from Muslim students in every year in the UESI movement.

3.3.4 Follow-up activities for the New Believers

UESI gives a lot of priority on mentoring students. It reiterates the senior graduates to be a role model in their lives. Daniel says, "Model life of the elders influences the new believers. Most of the UESI members have been model to me and I have been following in their footsteps by showing a model life in my work place. UESI is emphasizing on living like Christ."[188] Apart from this model life, the movement arranges systematic follow-up programs for the new believers. Vikram says, "We have taken the decision to plan and arrange at least two follow-up programs followed by an evangelistic program."[189] Chandra Shakar says, "In these follow-up meetings, they explain very clearly how to grow spiritually and how to live a new life."[190] Even though the movement is cautious about the follow-up activities, it is not up to the mark in this area. In his report in the Annual General body Meeting of UESI-AP, Vikram expresses, "I am very sorry to bring to your notice that in spite of many discussions we could not take interest for follow-up meetings."[191] Thus, there may be some problems in movement's follow-up work for the new believers.

Table 10: Follow-Up
SA-Strongly Agreed, AG-Agree, US-Unsure, DA-Disagree, SD-Strongly Disagree, NA-Not Answered

QQ	(n=120)	SA	AG	US	DA	SD	NA
20	The follow-up is more towards Christian background students comparing to other faiths	6%	53%	5%	34%	1.5%	0.5%
28	The follow-up is more towards Hindu background students comparing to other faiths	12%	44%	8%	31%	1.5%	3.5%
36	The follow-up is more towards Muslim background students comparing to other faiths	1.5%	8.5%	18%	53%	15%	4%

We can observe From the above table, that 59% of the respondents agreed with QQ 20. So we can say that a good follow-up is given for Christian background students. For QQ 28, 56% of the respondents agreed that the follow-up for the students from Hindu background is also good. There is only 3% of difference between the responses to QQ 20 & 28. It means that a good follow-up is given for Christian and Hindu background students and the follow-up is little bit more towards Christian background students. This may be one of the reasons that UESI consists of more number of Christian background students. This good follow-up may be one of the strong reasons for the significant impact of UESI on Christian and Hindu background believers.

A good number of 53% of the respondents has disagreed and 18% are unsure for the QQ 36. This indicates that follow-up towards Muslim background students might be poor. Perhaps there are a few Muslim background believers in the movement. This poor follow-up may be one of the strong reasons for the lack of leadership from Muslim background believers in the movement.

3.3.5 Majority of the Students from different backgrounds in number

Table 11: Majority students' background

a) 0-1%, b) 1-10%, c) 10-25%, d) 25-50%, e) 50-75%, f) 75-90%, g) 90-100, h) Not Answered

QQ	(n=120)	a	b	c	d	e	f	g	h
18	What is the percentage of students from Christian background in UESI ministry?	0	2	11	31	48	21	3	4
26	What is the percentage of students from Hindu background in UESI ministry?	3	26	26	34	20	8	0	3
34	What is the percentage of students from Muslim background in UESI ministry?	78	33	1	2	0	0	0	6

We have already come to a conclusion from the previous data analysis that, the percentage of Christian students is more in the movement than that of other faiths. This fact is again confirmed in the above table (11). For QQ 18 & 26, 21 respondents have agreed that there is 75% -90% Christian students in the movement whereas only 8 respondents agreed that there are 75-90% Hindu students in the movement. It is quite interesting to observe from the response to QQ 18 that 3 respondents expressed that Christian background believers' percentage in the movement is 90-100%. It gives a strong affirmation and confirmation that Christian background believers are significantly more in the movement. It means the movement's resources and efforts may be going more towards Christian students.

The 78 respondents agreed to QQ 34 that, there is only 0-1% Muslim students' presence in the movement. The encouraging response is that 33 respondents agreed that there is a 1-10% Muslim students in the movement. Since the scale is little long, it can be either 1% or 10%. In the light of above data analysis, there is no chance of having 10% Muslim students' presence in the movement. We can agree to 3% because we have already seen that there is 3% Muslim students' presence in the movement from QQ 1. Thus, the above table also affirms that there are a few followers of Christ from Muslim students, but they may not be stable enough to come to leadership. It indicates that the impact of UESI on them many not be effective.

3.3.6 Leadership Development

There is no doubt that UESI has made a significant impact on raising leaders to church and society. Its impact on producing quality leaders from Hindu students is noteworthy. In this context, M. Sudhakar speaks, "a number of Hindu students belonging to very orthodox and other kinds of Hindu backgrounds have also been coming to the Lord." He substantiates his statement from his own experience by saying, "my wife and I have seen many such people coming to know the Lord who are now faithful witnesses as tentmakers, missionaries, and people in the secular field but serving the Lord."[192]

3.3.6.1 Leadership Development for the Church
Table 12: Impact on Church
SA-Strongly Agreed, AG-Agree, US-Unsure, DA-Disagree, SD-Strongly Disagree, NA-Not Answered

QQ	(n=120)	SA	AG	US	DA	SD	NA
14	UESI has raised effective Leaders for the church from Christian students	38%	39%	9%	10%	2%	2%
22	UESI has raised effective Leaders for the church from Hindu students	16%	64%	13%	5%	0%	2%
30	UESI has raised effective Leaders for the church from Muslim students	2%	18%	33%	38%	5%	4%

The 38% of the respondents strongly agreed with QQ 14 that, the UESI has raised significant and effective leadership from Christian students. So, it is evident that the UESI has raised effective leaders for the church in India from Christian background students.

Another observation is that 80% (16+64) of the respondents, which is the majority in the table agreed that UESI has raised effective leaders for the church from Hindu students. This is supported by the words of Daniel. He says, "obviously Hindu students are taking leadership in the ministry." He further supports "all the EU (Evangelical Union) committee members of JNTU at present are from Hindu students. The President of EU is from Hindu, the Secretary is from BC, and the remaining committee members also are from Hindu background."[193] In fact, the findings from the above table seem to contradict the finding that has come from QQ 4 (Which religious background students are the majority in UESI leadership?) in Table: 6. The Majority of the people responded to QQ 4 that Christian students are more in UESI leadership. We understood from QQ 4 that UESI raised more leaders from Christian background students than other backgrounds but here the data gives an impression that Hindu background students' percentage in leadership is more compared to other faiths.

Analysis and Interpretation of Data

At the same time, if we observe the table very carefully there may not be any contradiction. The outcome for QQ 4, Christian students are more in leadership, can be affirmed if we take the percentage only under the column "Strongly Agreed." 38%, which is a significant percentage of respondents strongly agreed that UESI has raised effective leaders for the church from Christian students where as the response to QQ 22 informs that only 16% present of the respondents strongly agreed that the movement has raised effective leaders for the church from Hindu students. Thus, the outcome, Christian students are more in leadership, which come for QQ 4 can be trusted that the Christian students are more in leadership in the light of the above Table (12).

It is a known fact that, the impact of UESI on leadership development from Muslim students is very less. Since 2% strongly agreed that it has raised leaders to the church for QQ 30, there may be a rare cases in the movement but in a larger context its impact may be 0% because the outcome for QQ 3, 4 & 5 has informed us that the movement's impact in the area of leadership from Muslim students is 0%.

3.3.6.2 Leadership Development for the Society

Table 13: Impact on Society

SA-Strongly Agreed, AG-Agree, US-Unsure, DA-Disagree, SD-Strongly Disagree, NA-Not Answered

QQ	(n=120)	SA	AG	US	DA	SD	NA
15	UESI has raised effective Leaders for the society from Christian students	15%	48%	16%	17%	1%	3%
23	UESI has raised effective Leaders for the society from Hindu students	11%	51%	26%	9%	0.5%	2.5%
31	UESI has raised effective Leaders for the society from Muslim students	2%	15%	36%	38%	6%	3%

UESI has raised a significant number of leaders in society who have been influential in secular field. Students belong to different faiths have been influenced in this aspect. For QQ 15 a good number of 63% (15+48) which is majority in the table have agreed that UESI has raised effective leaders for the society from Christian students. Emmanuel Ratnaraj, one of the UESI members from Christian background, is an example to support this finding. UESI's In Touch, monthly news letter reports, "Thirteen students and one of the alumni led by our graduate Mr. Emmanuel Ratnaraj working in APEEJAY School, Jalandhar, Punjab, have won the International Space Shuttle Design Competition held at NASA's Johnson Space Center in Texas, USA."[194] This is just one of the examples from the numerous stories of UESI members' impact in the secular field as believers. There are hundreds of leaders from Christian background in the secular field as teachers, lectures, IAS officers, social workers and in several respective positions in the government as well as private and semi-government organizations.

In the same way, the impact of UESI on Hindu students in the field of producing leaders in society is also noteworthy. 62% (11+51) agreed for QQ 23 that it has produced leaders for the society. There is only 1% of difference of opinion between QQ 15 & 23. Thus, the impact of UESI on producing leaders from Christian and Hindu background in secular society is almost equal.

The interesting finding in QQ 31 is that 17% (2+15) of the respondents agreed that UESI raised effective leaders for the society from Muslim students. We may suspect that this 17% of the respondents did not understand the question clearly or they are not so conscious about answering the question because it contradicts with QQ 3, 4 & 5. Even personally, I haven't found any single leader from Muslim background who has been nurtured by UESI and working in a secular field; or the respondents may know of some.

3.3.7 Literature Development

Table 14: Literature Development

QQ	(n=120)	SA	AG	US	DA	SD	NA
16	UESI has developed helpful literature to reach Christian students	29%	59%	2%	8%	1%	1%
24	UESI has developed helpful literature to reach Hindu students	24%	48%	10%	16%	0%	2%
32	UESI has developed helpful literature to reach Muslim students	2%	37%	24%	30%	4%	3%

Literature is one of the main sources to impact the thinking of people. The above table informs us that UESI has developed literature to impact students of different faiths. The table helps us to understand that, its efforts on developing literature to impact Christian students is more than to impact other faiths because 88% (29+59) of the respondents in QQ 16 agreed that the movement has developed helpful literature to reach Christian students, whereas 72% (24+48) of the respondents of QQ 24 have agreed that it developed helpful literature to reach Hindu students and only 39% (2+37) have responded for QQ 32 that the movement developed literature to reach Muslim students.

Another observation is that, the table gives an impression to the reader that there is distinct literature for these three faith students but as far as my knowledge goes back there is no specific literature that was developed exclusively for students of different faiths. There was a little effort to produce different tracts for "Valentine's Day" and a tract entitled "Neegamyam (Your destiny)," which was meant for Non-Christians.[195] Apart from these little efforts, there has been no specially developed literature for different faiths but the respondents informed that UESI has developed literature for different faiths. There is an apparent contradiction here when we tally the response from QQs and interviews, thus what I suspect is that the respondents might have thought that these QQs 16, 24 & 32 meant general literature to influence all faiths. If it is so, the QQs should have been more specific to get the adequate information from the respondents which might have avoided this confusion.

3.3.8 Contextual Methods

Table 15: Contextual Methods

QQ	(n=120)	SA	AG	US	DA	SD	NA
17	UESI has developed culturally relevant and contextualized methods for Christian students	19%	53%	9%	13%	2%	4%
25	UESI has developed culturally relevant and contextualized methods for Hindu students	13%	50%	14%	15%	2%	6%
33	UESI has developed culturally relevant and contextualized methods for Muslim students	0.5%	26%	29%	36%	4%	4.5%

One of the observations from the data is that, the UESI is sensitive to the cultural issues of the students. In fact, the members of UESI approach the other faith students in a sensitive manner. For instance John Paul narrated to me his experience of relating with students of different faiths in Hyderabad Central University when he pioneered the work.

I went to Central University in 1988 there was no body interested in Bible Studies or spiritual things. I related myself with a few students who belong to different faiths and took them to outside gate of the University and sat with them in the lawn. I was sensitive to the context and started discussion on 'Existence of God' and finally discussion ended that there is a God. Before we depart I said let us pray, then immediately a student asked me, "To whom shall we pray?" I paused a moment and I said, "I pray in the name of the beginner." That gave them attraction and neutrality of our mind. We patiently waited, as the result ministry was started and it is continuing.[196]

The response from the respondents for QQ 17 indicates that UESI is more sensitive to the culture of Christian and Hindu background students compared to Muslim background students. 72% (19+53), a good percentage of respondents agreed that the movement has developed culturally relevant and contextualized methods for Christian background students. Since, the movement consist more number of Christian background students, it might be giving priority to them in developing relevant contextual methods.

In QQ 25, 63% (13+50) of the respondents agreed that the movement developed culturally relevant and contextual methods to reach Hindu background students. As a follower of Christ from Hindu background I can affirm that UESI's ministry methods are somewhat relevant to Hindu background students. When I accepted Christian faith in this movement I felt accepted because no one asked me to change my name or forced me to attend a Church. I was comfortable in sitting on the floor in a circle and singing devotional songs in my own language. I adjusted and felt at home in the fellowship because the "Bible Study Groups" resembled me just like Hindu bhajan groups in the temple. I use to sit in such bhajan groups in the temple and I found similar type of worship in a different context which made me to relax. Thus, UESI is somewhat relevant with Hindu students

The interesting observation from QQ 33 is that 29% were unsure, 36% disagreed and 4% strongly disagreed. These figures may indicate that UESI might not have succeeded in developing relevant and contextual methods for Muslim background students. In this context Ezekiel frankly admits that "the methods UESI uses for different faith students are same"[197] Muntaj also expressed that "there are no exactly relevant methods to reach Muslim students in UESI."[198] On the same issue, Sudhakar Rao, State Secretary of UESI-AP, frankly admitted that "there are no exactly culturally relevant and contextualized methods in reaching students of different faiths."[199] Thus, I suspect the data which says that there are contextual methods for students of different faiths.

Summary and Analysis

The facts that have come from RQ 3 show that the Christian background believers are little bit more in number compared to Hindu background students, but at the same time Hindu students are more influenced and they are active in the ministry. It is true that the movement made some impact on Hindu students but it may not be that much significant, because if we take Indian population, Hindus consist of 81.3% where as Christians are only 2.3% in records.[200] QQs should have been designed to assess the impact of UESI on students of different faiths in the light of distribution of population. If we analyze UESI's impact in the light of distribution of population, its impact might be very less on Hindus and its ministry may be happening mostly among 2.3% Christian population of the country.

Another factor is that the movement is lacking creative evangelistic efforts. Young people need creative approaches. In the context of Indian youth, Jacob G. Isaac has been practicing innovative methods such as "Kerygma Coffee House," "Kerygma Coffee Talks" on different youth-related issues which attract the students of other faiths.[201] The suggested "Hospitality" method in literature review can be seen in "1:3 discipling" strategy in the movement's follow-up methods.

The significant observation from the data is that, the UESI is lacking contextual approaches in its evangelistic efforts especially for Muslim students. The theory of contextualization, which has been discussed thoroughly in the precedent literature, has not been seen in mission practice of UESI. Contextualization of the Gospel is essential in evangelizing people of other faiths, because in this theory the "basic principle was to start where the person was in his own orientation to life."[202] Muslims may not be comfortable with the traditional way of Christian worship or religious practices which may be one of the reasons that the impact of UESI on Muslim students is 0%. It does not mean that there are no followers of Christ from Muslim students in the movement but the movement has not raised any effective leaders for the church and society from these students. The other point of view is that, Muslim students who have come to

Analysis and Interpretation of Data 77

the Lord may not be attentive in spiritual matter. Whatever the reason it might be, the movement's impact on Muslim students is 0%.

Lack of adequate literature to reach the students of other faiths is a gap in the movement's Evangelistic efforts. In fact literature plays a vital role in evangelization. George Verwer reminds a statement made by Mahatma Gandhi's nephew who said, "The missionaries have taught us read, but the Communists have given us the literature."[203] Printing material has such a power to influence people but it is a fact that the Christian literature that can influence people of other faiths in Indian context is less. In this context Aghamkar found out in his research related to the ministry to Hindus in Pune City that the literature that can influence Hindus is less.[204] It has been observed that this problem is not only in UESI, but the problem of the Indian church that it has not developed adequate literature in Indian context. It is very hard to touch the preconceived minds of students who are from other faiths, but the adequate literature can do that. Even though there are a few believers in the UESI from Muslim background, the movement has failed to encourage them to come to leadership positions in the church. One of the reasons suggested by the data is that the movement may not be giving appropriate follow-up to these new believers. The movement raised effective leaders from Christian and Hindu students for the church and society, but developing leaders from Muslim students is 0%. One more possibility from the data is that the movement may not be using relevant and contextual approaches to impact Muslim students. Since culture creates walls that do not allow the individual to grow in new found faith Parshall's C4 model can be a great help to relate with Muslim students.[205]

3.4 Hindrances, Effective methods and Strategies to reach the Students of all Faiths

This section mainly focuses on the hindrances that the movement has been facing and the effective outreach methods and strategies applying to evangelize the students of all different faiths. One of the suspected hindrances is that the movement's attention to reach other faiths might be less or the zeal for evangelism may be lacking. In this connection, the recent report of UESI's AGM reports "it is observed that our efforts are going into comfort zone (Believers retreats, fellowship, open home etc.). It is high time to refocus on evangelism."[206] Since the ministry has grown so much, obviously the movement's focus may be shifting from evangelism to other administrative and fellowship matters by neglecting its core aim - evangelism.

RQ 4. What strategies and implementation plans would help this organization evolve a better ministry among students of all three faiths?

3.4.1 Hindrances for Evangelizing Students of different Faiths
Table 16: Hindrances

1. Fear, 2. No Burden, 3. No Appropriate Literature, 4. No Time, 5. Not equipped, 6. Any other 7. Not Answered

QQ		1	2	3	4	5	6	7
38	What are the possible hindrances to share the Gospel to nominal Christian students? (n=165)	17%	34%	11%	9%	17%	4%	8%
42	What are the possible hindrances to share the Gospel to Hindu students? (n=177)	24%	22%	17%	6%	25%	3%	3%
46	What are the possible hindrances to share the Gospel to Muslim students? (n=183)	34%	16%	22%	2%	20%	2%	4%

Is has been examined from the responses to QQ 38, that the 34% of the respondents have agreed that, the major hindrance to evangelize Christian students is lacking burden towards them. Lack of burden is the major hindrance to reach these students because other problems like fear, literature and the skills to share the Gospel may not be a big problem.

Analysis and Interpretation of Data 79

According to QQ 42, 25% of the respondents, which is the highest opinion of the people, expressed that the members of UESI are not equipped. Another hindrance can be fear that is why 24% expressed this concern. There are a few valuable observations under the column "Any other" in this QQ 42. A. Vijaya Kumar noted "so called 'WIDE MINDED'" as one of the problems in reaching Hindu students.[207] What I suspect his intended meaning in this phrase is that Hindus are pluralistic thinkers in their pursuit of truth. This is the major hindrance with the Hindus because it's very hard for them to accept the exclusive claims of Christ. Jaya Kumar agrees to this statement and he says, "Probably the most common Hindu objection to Christianity is that Christians believe that there is only one way to God."[208] Another valuable comment given by Satish, an EU student, is that "not able to continue them 100%."[209] What he meant can be that UESI is not able to help them to continue in the faith. Obviously it happens, if there is no proper care and follow-up for the new believers from Hindu background.

The major problem expressed in reaching Muslim students in QQ 46 is quite different from other faiths. "Fear" is the major hindrance to reach Muslims because 23%, which is the majority respondents' opinion in QQ 46. A careful observation of the above table informs us that the hindrance "Fear" is gradually increased from QQ 38 to QQ 46. In this context, M. Sudhakar comments "the common slogan we hear from Christians is that it's very difficult to evangelize Muslims, and my view on this is that they even really don't try to evangelize and even without trying to evangelize, they go with this preconceived notion." He further makes a radical statement saying, "Most of the Christians are scared of Muslims because of the questions."[210] Ezekiel, an EGF member, also frankly admits, "Our students could not able to go and share the Gospel with Muslims because of the fear."[211] Usually Muslims raise some of the critical theological questions such as Trinity, Son of God, Divinity of Jesus, Resurrection of Christ and the canon of the Bible. Since some of these questions are hard to answer, people are scared to share the Gospel with them.

In fact, usually believers are biased towards Muslims to some extent and they are not willing to share the Gospel with them. Pasha, an EU student from Muslim background, says, "Usually people think that Muslims don't listen and also they get afraid of Muslims. At least if they share, some may not listen but surely some will listen but believers are not willing to share the Gospel with them."[212] Thus, unwillingness with preconceived notion might be another hindrance to reach Muslim students.

QQ 46 informs us that lack of adequate literature is the second highest opinion from the respondents in the area of possible hindrances to share the Gospel to Muslim students. It may be true that UESI did not give much attention to develop adequate literature to evangelize them. This finding can be confirmed from the above previous Table: 14, which revealed that the movement's concentration on developing relevant literature to reach Muslim background students is less.

3.4.2 Effective method of Evangelism

The following three questions QQ 39, 43 & 47 are open ended questions, but the respondents have very clearly mentioned their opinions which come under different well known evangelistic methods and strategies. It's amazing to see how different people have agreed on the same subject. All the answers are categorically divided under different sections, if there are any answers that are not fitting under these categories they are explained in the narration under the column "Any other".

QQ 39: Which is the most effective method of evangelism to nominal Christian students?

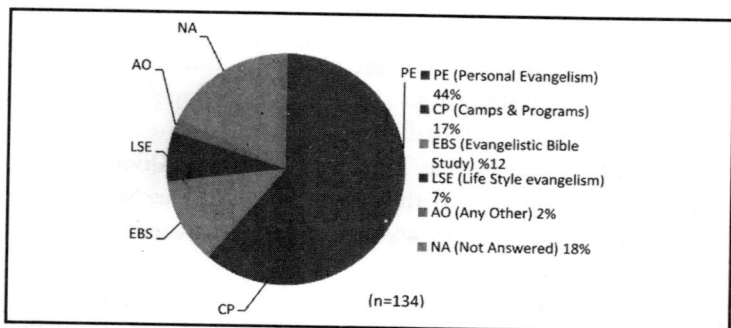

Figure 3: Effective methods for Christian students

Analysis and Interpretation of Data

In this part, different effective methods which have been practiced are discussed. Forty four percent of the respondents suggested Personal Evangelism is an effective method of evangelism to reach Christian students. In fact, any student will be attracted to the Gospel in personal evangelism. This method is effective to deal with these students who "take the Gospel casually." Another factor is that these students think "they know everything and they don't accept easily."[213] I think the respondents are aware of this problem that is why they gave significant preference to Personal Evangelism.

The second priority is given by the respondents is Camps and Programs. Camps and programs are other attractive methods, UESI has been using in its evangelistic activities among Christian students. 7% of the respondents suggested Life Style evangelism, what they expressed in writing is that "believers should live an exemplary life to attract other nominal Christian students to the fellowship." One person, Emmanuel Subhakar, has suggested "Musical Evenings" which I kept in the column "Any Other."

QQ 43: Which is the most effective method of Evangelism to the Hindu Students

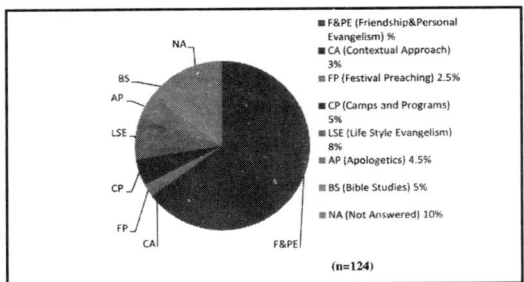

Figure 4: Effective methods for Hindu students

Friendship and personal evangelism is the most effective evangelistic method that was proposed by the respondents to reach Hindu students. Friendship is one of the most essential gifts needed by any evangelist to relate with people of other faiths especially to Hindus. David Jaya Kumar says, "Friendship Evangelism is usually easy to initiate with Hindus. Most Hindus esteem religion in general and are free and open to speak about it. A consistently Christ-like life is the most important factor in sharing the Gospel with Hindus."[214] In this friendship evangelism "we should give top priority to the personal aspect of evangelism in order to be effective. We should develop such good friendship with people that we can talk to them freely about anything (including spiritual matters) and we can engage them in a sustained dialogue."[215] Then life style evangelism is given second priority which is also a part of Friendship and Personal Evangelism.

UESI gives lot of importance to personal life-style that impacts students whom they mentor. Tina Thomas says, "Besides learning lessons through classes, we learnt many important lessons by seeing the exemplary lifestyles of staff and graduates."[216] In fact, "many Non-Christian converts' life style impacted other Non-Christians."[217] Many Non-Christians, especially Hindus get attracted to the Gospel because of model lives in the campuses. For instance, M. Sudhakar who made a great impact in Osmania University during his student days, recollects his campus life and says, "By God's grace, throughout my student career in Osmania, I maintained my Christian identity very clear, as a Christian I took active role in the affairs of the campus life and also witnessed Christ with my model life. As the result, by the time I finished my M.Sc praise be to the Lord, we had four "Bible Study Groups" in different Hostels on the University campus."[218] Thus, Lifestyle Evangelism is one of the effective methods to reach Hindu students.

QQ 47: Which is the most effective method of Evangelism to the Muslim students?

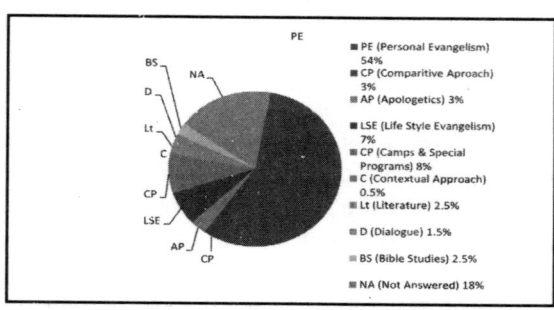

Figure 5: Effective methods for Muslim students

A good number of 54% respondents suggested Personal Evangelism and 7% suggested Lifestyle Evangelism which is a part of Personal Evangelism as an effective method of evangelism to the Muslim students. This is the best approach to relate with students of any faith, students that is why UESI insists its members "giving special emphasis to personal evangelism, for effective evangelism."[219]

The next priority given by the respondents after Personal Evangelism is conducting camps and special programs. 8% respondents suggested this strategy but the problem is "Muslim students' attendance in UESI's evangelistic programs is very less, but even if they attend they generally come with a set of questions with an intention to raise against Christian faith and most of those questions are related to Trinity, reliability of the Bible, deity of Jesus."[220]

In the case of outreach to Christian and Hindus background students Bible study method was given some priority (12% suggested Bible study method" to reach Christian students in Figure 3, 5% suggested Bible study method to reach Hindu students in Figure 4) but in the case of outreach to Muslims students only 2.5% of the respondents suggested this method. This response may mean that the traditional Bible study method may not be sufficient to win students from Muslim background students. In fact, socially Muslims are encouraged not to respect the Bible which is why there should be some change in method of conducting bible studies to the Muslim background students. Muntaj, an EU student from Muslim background says, "It is better to organize special Bible studies and programs exclusively for Muslim background students because they will not feel comfortable in mixed group. So my opinion is that there should be separate teaching initially, but after some maturity and clarity those students can be mixed with other students."[221] I did not find any evidence in my interaction with the people that UESI conducts separate Bible studies for Muslim background students.

Dialogue is another suggestion that came from the data. Sudhakar suggests that "closed room dialogues"[222] and debates will help the Muslims to think rightly because most of the intellectual "Muslims are influenced and received a set of questions by Ahmed Deedad, Zachir Nayak, local Islamic apologists and dava preachers. Most of those questions make Christians disarmed and defenseless."[223]

Thus, closed room dialogues may help these students to understand the truth in Christian faith.

3.4.3 Effective follow-up

Table 17: Suggested effective follow-up

1. 1:3 Discipling, 2. Friendship, 3. Financial help, 4. Help in their career, 5. Any other, 6. Not Answered

QQ		1	2	3	4	5	6
40	What kind of follow-up is needed to Christian background students (n=177)	46%	26%	4%	19%	2%	3%
44	What kind of follow-up is needed to Hindu background students (n=195)	24%	44%	9%	20%	1%	2%
48	What kind of follow-up is needed to Muslim background students? (n=190)	23%	46%	8%	17%	1%	5%

The majority of the respondents, 46%, suggested that "1:3 Discipling,"[224] method is needed in giving effective follow-up for Christian students in QQ 40. K. Sudhakar Rao, the State Secretary of UESI, explained to me about this "1:3 Discipling" follow-up method in my interview with him. He said, "One senior EU student and two junior students who accepted the Lord recently accompanied with an EGF member meet frequently for prayer and fellowship apart from the regular Bible studies and programs." He further mentioned, "This follow-up method has been giving effective results in UESI-AP."[225] The EGF member, who is the mentor in every "1:3 Discipling" follow-up group, takes care of the students' spiritual life.

QQ 44 and 48 in the table inform us that "friendship" is the most effective follow-up to Hindu and Muslim students. This follow-up method, and friendship, is somewhat different to "1:3 Discipling." "1:3 Discipling" method functions like a cell group in which at least three different ages and experience people (senior

EU student, new follower of Christ and an elderly EGF members." This follow-up may not be significantly effective because there may be age and experience and cultural difference to mentor high caste Hindu and Muslim background believers. This may be reason the responders gave priority to friendship method of follow-up these background students.

Under the column "Any Other" G. Krishna Reddy, an EGF member, suggested "Personal Care" is needed in order to have an effective follow-up to the Christian background students.[226] Reddy's comment is noteworthy because personal care for the new believers helps them to be mature in new found faith. Another important suggestion given by G. Rajesh Babu is "Listening to them and sharing their problems."[227] This need of listening and sharing their problems also can be fulfilled if there is a proper care for the new believers in the fellowship.

3.4.4 Effective Strategy

Table 18: Strategy

1. Appointing a staff, 2. Special Programs, 3. Special training to believers, 4. Separate Annual budget, 5. Special prayer awareness, 6. Developing special literature, 7. Any other, 8. Not Answered

QQ	1	2	3	4	5	6	7	8
41. What should be the strategy for evangelizing Christian background students? (n=203)	7%	26%	24%	2%	23%	11%	3%	4%
45. What should be the strategy for evangelizing Hindu students? (n=226)	9%	28%	21%	3%	16%	19%	1%	3%
49. What should be the strategy for evangelizing Muslim students? (n=243)	10%	24%	23%	4%	19%	16%	1%	3%

The interesting suggestion from the data is that students need special programs irrespective of their religious background. We can see the majority of the respondents in all the three QQs in the table suggested "Special programs" as effective strategy to reach all these three faiths. This observation indicates that special programs are needed for particular faith background students. Traditionally UESI may not give special consideration to the students' religious background; instead same programs will be organized for all faith students. This fact is proven in the previous Table: 7. There is a common assumption from most of the members which makes them believe, "what these people are doing is sufficient to reach any kind of faith background students."[228] Because of this kind of thinking there may not be an attempt to develop specially designed different programs for different faith students. Another interpretation can be that the respondents might have suggested special programs which are relevant to all three faiths. In fact, the QQs are not emphasizing strategy exclusively meant for that particular religious faith.

Column No.5 (Special prayer awareness) gives an important insight to the reader. The respondents were more cautious about "Special Programs" because the majority of people's opinion is expressed to this strategy but less percentage of the respondents suggested "Special prayer awareness" as an effective strategy in reaching Hindu and Muslim students. 16% of the respondents suggested "Special prayer awareness" in QQ 45 to reach Hindu students, which is 4th position out of six suggested strategies. In the same way respondents selected "Special prayer awareness" as 3rd option to reach Muslim background students in QQ 49. This response from the members of the movement clearly indicates that people are not giving importance to the prayer instead they are more interested on programs.

It seems the respondents have not given that much priority to the strategy of appointing a specialized staff to reach particular faith students, because only 2% in Q 41, 3% in QQ 45 and 4% in QQ 49 responded to this strategy in the above table.

Summary and Analysis

Some of the major hindrances are lack of effective methods and strategies are revealed from the investigations to QQ 4. Lack of burden is the major hindrance to reach Christian students, apart from the minor hindrances such as fear, lack of literature and lack of time. In fact, "evangelism is a love driven process."[229] The love for lost souls and the evangelistic zeal will be reduced when we "replace our focus on eternity with a desire for comfort."[230] Out of many hindrances to reach students of other faiths, fear is the major factor that arrests the believers in their encounter with Hindu and Muslim students.

In order to be effective witnesses among Muslims, "Christians need to overcome stumbling blocks such as fear of Islam and Muslims, their own prejudices, and their lack of faith that Muslims can come to faith in Christ."[231] In fact believers are afraid of Muslims because of the questions they raise. This may indicate that the members need proper training and they need to be equipped to reach Muslims. Closed room dialogues with Muslims can bring some results because "dialogue is not only preparatory to witness, it is also the means to witness."[232] This is an effective method of witness among Muslims which is lacking in UESI ministry.

Personal Evangelism is the most effective method of evangelism to all three faiths suggested by the respondents. It is a dynamic method because it "looks for an opportunity to share the Gospel with someone" and it involves "relationship building" in which people will be ministered.[233] This topic is thoroughly discussed under the analysis of RQ 1.

Friendship is the most effective follow-up for nurturing Hindu and Muslim new followers of Christ because it helps in "identifying with them."[234] The data also suggests this method to give effective follow-up. Friendship helps the new comers feel at home and they learn more and in fact, unless they find deeper level of friendship from the group they may not continue in the fellowship.[235] It is evident that there are a few followers of Christ from Muslims, but the movement has not have impact on them in bringing them into leadership to the church and society. The suspected reason is that there may not be proper care and follow-up for these Muslim background believers.

The data shows that the UESI members may not be aware of the contextual approaches that are discussed in literature review, because there is only one person out of 120 suggested that "we should learn Urdu and be contextual" with their culture and customs in QQ 47. Another fact can be assumed that UESI members may be having negative attitude towards contextual approaches that prevail in the context of outreach to Muslims.

The reason for making this assumption is that one of the prominent UESI leaders from Hyderabad responded negatively to the QQ 17, 25 & 33 which are designed to find out whether UESI has developed contextual methods to reach students of different faiths. He circled these QQs with a red ink and wrote very clearly "It is not necessary at all," "Irrelevant and meaningless questions." Thus, we see some kind of negative preconceived notion towards contextual approaches to reach Muslim students.

The respondents suggested "Special programs" as the effective strategy to reach these three faiths while neglecting the necessity of prayer as a strategy. In this context Sami Dagher, one of the resource persons of Amsterdam 2000 Workshops, rightly evaluates the present trend in our evangelistic endeavor and says, "We have substituted the prayer and power of God, which is given to us, for programs."[236] The main reason for this trend is that we think "with new methods and programs we would have a successful ministry."[237] This is true in every mission organization in these days and UESI also falls into this trend. The data indicate that UESI uses the same programs for all faiths and there are no specially designed programs for different faith background students. Another observation is that we don't find John Travis' C_5 contextual method in the movement, which was discussed in Chapter Two.[238] This might be one of the reasons that UESI has not made much impact on Muslim background students.

Chapter Four

Recommendations and Conclusions

Introduction
The major focus of this chapter is to present some of the significant recommendations in the light of conclusions that are arrived from the in-depth analysis of the data. The First Chapter of the thesis has dealt with the problem and the research methodology. The Second Chapter has explored the precedent literature related to the topic which has mainly addressed mission to Hindus and Muslims in general and University students in particular. Various theories and mission practices have been discussed. The Third Chapter has presented the data that has been collected from the field and analyzed it in the light of precedent literature. The present Fourth Chapter is an outcome of the research.

4.1 Theological/Biblical Reflection
The major concern of this thesis is to find out the missionary work among the University students and explore some ways for raising witness effectively among the students of other faiths who

are not exposed to the Gospel and those who are outside of the Church. Often they are called gentiles by the Christians.. The new followers of Christ from other faiths are suspected in the fellowship. Sometimes, Christians resist in relating with people of other faiths and the negative thinking about people of other faiths may cause lack of witness among them. If we look into the scriptures, God has concern for all human beings irrespective of different religions, and His "Mission lies at the core of theology within the character and action of God Himself."[239] His concern for people of other faiths can be seen in the whole Bible, and the Scriptures clearly "reveal His redemptive purpose for the nations."[240] In fact "God's concern for all His people is clearly revealed in the Pentateuch, the first five books of the Bible."[241] God selected Abraham, an idolater, to be a blessing to the nations and He was always interested on people of other faiths to reveal His glory through His chosen nation "Israel." In this connection, Hedlund makes it so simple to understand that "what God does in Israel, becomes God's witness to the nations and reveals His redemptive activity to the worldwide audience."[242] For instance God's mighty acts in Babylon revealed His glory. The King Nebuchadnezzar confessed to Daniel, "Surely your God is the God of Gods and the Lord of Kings…" (Dan 2:46). He also acknowledged God's power and said, "I praised the Most High; I honored and glorified him who lives forever" (Dan 4:34). The story of Jonah is an example to understand God's concern for people of other faiths (Jonah 4:11).

The early church struggled to incorporate Gentiles into the church. Initially, they did not understand God's concern for Gentiles - people of other faiths. The Lord had to deal with Peter in a spectacular way through a vision to help them to understand His plan of salvation for the people of other faiths (Acts 10). New Testament records that "the early church valued an intensive, aggressive evangelization of all people: both Jews and Gentiles."[243] In fact, it is God's will that every tribe, language, people and nation should worship Him. The high-caste Hindu and Muslim students are yet to be reached with the Gospel. God desires their presence in His Kingdom which demands our undivided attention to extend His love to them, so that they realize and are attracted to the King of

Kings, Christ Jesus. In this context, UESI needs to extend its mission to students of other faiths.

4.2 Recommendations from the Research Questions

4.2.1 First Research Question: Ministry methods

Contextual methods related to reaching Hindus in general and Muslims in particular should be adopted by the movement in its evangelistic activities for the effectiveness of the witness. The traditional approaches that are relevant to Christian students may not be sufficient to reach other faith students. Thus, the movement should adopt and practice relevant contextual methods. Creative and contextual methods that are appropriate and relevant to students of other faiths need to be discovered and implemented in evangelizing them. The constituency of the UESI needs to study and explore culturally relevant methods that can attract Hindu and Muslim students. The negative notion of incorporating new approaches and contextual methods should be replaced with positive mind in witnessing to students of others faiths. Since the UESI came into existence from Western Student Movements, there is always a tendency to bring western methodology into Indian mission field.

Traditional methods such as Group Bible Studies, Camps, Gospel evenings, Christmas Evangelistic Programs need to be modified in the context of Indian culture, keeping orthodox Hindu and Muslim students in mind. There is always a tendency to be satisfied with what the movement has been doing with its traditional methods which are relevant to the Christian students on the Indian campuses. The movement needs to think beyond Christian students to reach other faiths with adequate, relevant and contextual methods.

Separate programs need to be designed to reach students of other faiths. The movement should appoint a research-team who can study, investigate and design separate programs for non-Christians. In this context the movement should do an in-depth analysis of its programs and their effectiveness among students of other faiths. A research oriented team is essential in the movement to implement new programs and strategies to reach students of other faiths.

Creating awareness and importance of reaching students of other faiths are lacking in the movement, which demands serious attention to educate EUs and EGFs in grass-root level. Another factor is that the burden for reaching other faiths should be germinated in every member of the organization. Camps, conferences and believers' gatherings can be platforms to bring awareness of reaching students of other faiths.

Special training should be given to Christian students and they should be equipped with skills to reach high-caste Hindus and Muslims. Since the movement consists of Christian students more, there will be a tendency to develop Christian culture which may not be suitable to other faith students. Thus, these Christian students need to be trained in a proper manner to relate with the students of other faiths.

Personal Evangelism is the most effective method of evangelism to Christian, Hindu and Muslim background students. The movement should find out a creative mechanism that can help all the members to employ in personal evangelism. Personal Evangelism should be given priority in reaching the students of other faiths. The members of the movement should be equipped with different skills like: interpersonal communication skills, making new friends, social networking, making friends at playground, or on travel, and different methods of Personal Evangelism to engage in Personal Evangelism in a creative way. In order to practice Personal Evangelism, the movement should seriously evaluate the present trends in the ministry which have become program oriented by neglecting one of the core values of the movement: Personal Evangelism.

Festivals of other faiths can be used as occasions for social gathering to present the Gospel. It is a good thing to notice that the movement has been presenting the Gospel to students of other faiths by using Christmas as a special occasion, at the same time, festivals of Hindus and Muslims also can be considered as occasions to witness Christ. In his research, F. C. Beicho observed a nonthreatening approach with Hindus by "Evangelical Church of Maraland among the Tiwa tribes of Assam," (ECM) which can be adopted. Beicho narrates, "During the time of festivals, the missionaries would attend. They would then share the Good News to the people."[244] Usually, the

UESI members invite students of other faiths to participate in their Christmas celebration and they share the Gospel. It will be good if the members are encouraged to attend festivals of other faiths to build meaningful relationships through which they can share the Gospel.

The followers of Christ from other faiths should be equipped and trained to reach their own communities because "students witnessing to students" is one of the outstanding strategies that can be effective in college campuses. There are a few high-caste Hindu and Muslim followers of Christ in the movement. They should be adopted and trained by the movement to reach their own community.

4.2.2 Second Research Question: Response towards the Gospel

Middle class students of other faiths are quite positive to the Gospel. Thus, what the movement can do is that, these middle class Hindu students can be focused in evangelistic efforts and they can be used to reach orthodox Hindu students. The followers of Christ from these middle class should be equipped to reach high class Hindu students because middle class Hindus are accepted by them. The receptivity of the Gospel by high-caste Hindu students will be good if the movement uses middle class followers of Christ in evangelizing them.

Preconceived notions about Muslims should be clarified to the members of the movement, especially negative thinking which makes them to believe "Muslim students are a different kind of group because they never open to any kind of teaching except Islam."[245] This is a wrong notion that hinders people from engaging in witnessing to Muslims. In order to remove these preconceived notions, members of the movement should be educated through special seminars, lectures and teaching sessions in their Bible study groups.

Muslim students may not respond to the Gospel easily, but surely there will be some response if we communicate the Gospel in a way that they receive it. In fact, if we share the Gospel according to the context of their culture and religion, surely there may be some people who respond to the Gospel. One good thing about the student community is that they listen to the message which is my experience. When Paul preached to the intellectual people of Athens, people heard him and the majority of them were not interested to accept his message, but from the same crowd there were a few who accepted his teaching (Acts 17: 18-34). In the same way, surely there will be some students who give a positive response to the Gospel if the Gospel is preached in such a way that they get attracted to it.

4.2.3 Third Research Question: Impact of UESI on Students of different Faiths

Follow-up activities for the new followers of Christ from other faiths need to be strengthened. The movement needs to develop a special follow-up mechanism to mentor them. In order to be effective in giving follow-up for them, the movement should make an adequate survey to gather the facts about struggles and difficulties of high-caste Hindu and Muslim believers and it should develop appropriate methods and techniques to nurture them in spiritual life, so that they become stable and get maturity so as to come up to leadership level.

Genuine love and patience is needed to mentor the students of other faiths. The followers of Christ from other faiths, especially high-caste Hindu and Muslim students, have to go through lot of struggles. The so-called believers in the church suspect them, and their own society rejects them, especially the Muslim students face lot of persecution and danger of death. In such situations, the member of the movement should extend their genuine love, care, hospitality and help in every aspect of their needs in terms of financial, moral, and psychological. The new believers from Hindu and Muslim community come with lot of cultural beliefs and practices along with socio and religious notions that may trouble them. Thus, "genuine love for them" can motivate these new believers to come to spiritual maturity in the Lord; otherwise they may not be stable in the faith. Personal care and love is essential for spiritual maturity for the new followers of Christ of any faith.

Special programs are lacking in the movement to reach the students of other faiths. The Evangelism Department should conduct at least two programs in a year exclusively for Hindu students, and only Hindu students should be invited for these programs. It will be good if the speaker is selected from the follower of Christ from high-caste who can share the Gospel from his own experience. The students will be receptive to the Gospel in such programs.

In the same manner, programs exclusively for Muslims should be conducted at least once or twice in a year. An expert in evangelizing Muslims should be assigned as resource person preferably a follower of Christ from the same background. As far as my knowledge is concerned, there was no such program conducted in UESI-AP. Thus, special programs should be initiated for effective response from students of other faiths.

Leadership from students of other faiths should be raised. Since there are some followers of Christ from orthodox Hindu and Muslim background, these students should be trained in leadership skills. They should be given preference in leadership especially to reach students of their same faith. In order to see some fruit among Muslim students, the movement needs to keep some efforts in nurturing Muslim believers and they should be given leadership positions. It has been identified that there is not any single field- staff from Muslim background in its 55 years of long history. Unless, the movement focuses on developing leaders for Christ from this Islamic background, it is not possible to impact this community. Thus, this is the time for the movement to seriously think about the matter and to have long term goals and strategies to raise leaders from Muslim believers.

Literature that can attract students of other faiths need to be published. Since, there are a good number of writers in the movement, they should be encouraged to write tracts and booklets related to reach students of other faiths. In fact, literature plays a vital role in evangelism especially in the context of reaching Hindus and Muslims, but there are no relevant tracts that can attract the students of other faiths. There is no single Urdu tract with UESI which can be a great help to witness to them. So, the movement needs to publish adequate tracts in their own language to be effective in its mission to other faiths.

4.2.4 Fourth Research Question: Hindrances and Effective methods

Burden and passion for evangelizing students of other faiths should be generated among the members of UESI. Since Christian students may not take the Gospel seriously, they should be targeted separately and it is better if they are not mixed with other faith students. The movement should maintain a good rapport with local churches to train these Christian students.

Fear of Muslims should be replaced with courage in the minds of UESI members to engage in evangelizing Muslim students. Fear is the major hindrance and preconceived notion that is hindering the members from engaging in witnessing to Muslim students on the campuses. This preconceived notion should be replaced with courage by providing the members with to witness Muslim students.

Dialogue method of evangelism needs to be initiated in evangelistic efforts with students of other faiths especially in dealing with Muslims. The monologue preaching methods may not satisfy the students of other faiths. Preaching should be in dialogue form in which students of other faiths can engage in expressing their views. The traditional type of monologue preaching needs to be modified. Thus, the important suggestion is that the members need to be equipped with thorough knowledge of beliefs and practices of other faiths and trained with appropriate contextual methods to reach them.

The appointment of a specially trained staff to reach Muslim background students is the need of the hour in the UESI movement. The concern for developing special programs can be fulfilled when there is a specially trained staff who can initiate to reach Hindu and Muslim students. Even though UESI has a long history of 55 years, there hasn't any single staff worker been appointed to reach exclusively Muslim students. Usually UESI staff is over burdened with huge geographical location of the field and organizational responsibilities. Even though the staff may have the concern to reach neglected Muslim students, they cannot concentrate due to overload on them. Thus, the major concern to reach Muslim background students can be addressed by appointing a specially trained staff in the field, preferably a Muslim background believer. His presence may bring some results in reaching students of Islamic faith. The respondents have not given much priority to this suggestion in Table: 18. It suggests that the members of UESI are not strategically thinking in the context of evangelizing Muslim students which might be another reason that its impact on Muslim students is less. Suppose if there is a staff meant for reaching Muslim students, obviously he will bring awareness in the movement and the special programs will be initiated.

Special Prayer awareness to reach the students of other faiths should be initiated in the movement. Prayer should be the first priority in reaching them. The movement should encourage, enlighten and enforce all of its members to engage in constant prayer to break the strong holds of the evil one. Prayer walks can be conducted in Hindu and Muslim colonies to see the result. Silent prayer walks around the college campuses can bring effective results because I have seen tremendous result through this strategy in my ministry among high-caste Hindu students in the state of Uttarakhand. All night prayers can be conducted exclusively to pray for students of other faiths focusing on some colleges and universities.

Missionary students[246] should be motivated to take courses in some of the untouched Muslim Universities in the country. There is no Christian witness in some of the Universities such as The Jamia Millia Islamia University, Delhi; The Jamia Markazu University near Calicut; Aligarh Muslim University, UP. There are hundreds of college campuses across the country in which Christian presence is nil. The matured Christian students should be motivated to take courses in such colleges to establish Christian witness. The same strategy should be adopted in establishing Christian students witness in orthodox Hindu college campuses.

There are some university and college campuses dominated by high-caste Hindus. There is no Christian presence in many of such colleges and universities. Usually Christian students tend to join in Christian colleges to get good fellowship, Christian culture and atmosphere. In fact, Christian parents tend to seek admission for their children in Christian colleges thinking they will be spoiled if they get admitted in Non-Christian colleges. Matured believing students should be challenged to go as missionary students to these Hindu and Muslim Universities.

For instance, most of the Christian students in Guntur district of Andhra Pradesh seek admission for higher education in "Andhra Christian College", which was established by missionaries, where as next to this college there is another college named "Hindu College." In the same city, there is a Muslim minority college named "Andhra Muslim College" which is open for students of all faiths. There has been EU ministry for decades in Andhra Christian College, but there is no witness in Hindu college or in Andhra Muslim College. No one bothers about it. This is just an example in one city, but the same trend can be found in almost all the cities in the country. EU students should scatter to untouched colleges to establish witness among students of other faiths.

4.3 Recommendation for further research

This research is just a foretaste in the context of Christian mission among students of different faiths limited to the UESI ministry in Hyderabad Universities. Since there is no adequate research in the area of Christian mission to students of other faiths, this research can be a base to start further research to explore the new avenues to impact the untouched high-caste Hindu and Muslim students of India particularly and other nations generally.

One of the needy areas for further study could be social analysis of Muslim students' trends in Indian universities and their struggles so that we may know their needs to present the Gospel in a realistic manner. Since, UESI has been struggling to stabilize the students' ministry in North India, on the basis of the present research, it will be appropriate to encourage someone to take up an in-depth study of reaching Hindu students in North Indian universities so that it can help the ministry to grow in North India.

Summary and Conclusion

God's concern for all human beings is revealed in His Scriptures. It is God's will that people of all religions should know Him and experience His gift of salvation. He is not partial in His mission but rather He is at work in attracting people of all faiths. We see God's amazing revelation to people of other faiths in the Old Testament as well as in the New Testament. Initially, the early church did not understand God's universality in His plan of salvation but Peter's personal encounter with God in a vision made the church to accept gentiles into the church. The Christian mission agencies and churches in India need to develop love and compassion to extend His love towards the neglected.

In this context, UESI's ministry should expand its efforts to reach Hindu and Muslim students. It needs to develop contextual methods which will be relevant to Indigenous religious beliefs and practices. The followers of Christ from other faiths especially from high-caste Hindu and Muslim students should be trained to reach their own communities.

The new followers of Christ from other faiths should be given adequate follow-up to see them coming up into leadership. Concentration on developing special programs and relevant literature for students of other faiths should be improved.

Prayer awareness for students of other faiths should be initiated. Prayer should be given first priority to see fruitful results. Silent prayer walks around Hindu and Muslim colleges should be planned and initiated. Matured believing students should be challenged and motivated to take admissions in Hindu and Muslim colleges to establish Christian witness.

There is a great need for further research that can help the movement to extend its ministry to high-caste Hindus and Muslims in the Indian universities; especially research is needed to find out effective ways in its ministry in the context of reaching North Indian Hindu students.

References

1. Francis-Vincent Anthony, Hris A. M. Hermas and Carlsterkens, "Interpreting Religious Pluralism: Comparative Research Among Christian, Muslim and Hindu students in Tamil Nadu, India." *Journal of Empirical Theology* 18/2 (2005), 154.
2. Paul G. Hiebert, "The Christian Response to Hinduism," in *Missiology for the 21st Century*, edited by Roger E. Hedlund and Paul Joshua Bhakiaraj (New Delhi: ISPCK, 2004), 335.

3   Carin Zissis, "India's Muslim Population," *Council on Foreign Relations.* http://www.cfr.org/publication/13659/ (1st Feb 2009).
4   Atul Y. Aghamkar, *Insights into openness: Encouraging urban mission* (Bangalore: SAIACS Press, 2000), 144.
5   A. P. J. Abdul Kalam and Y S Rajan, *India 2020: A Vision for the New Millennium* (New Delhi: Penguin Books, 1998), 17.
6   NA, "The Great Indian Retail Story," Ernst & Young Pvt. Ltd, 2006. http://www.ey.com/Global/assets.nsf/Sweden/The_Great_Indian_Retail_Story/$file/The%20Great%20Indian%20Retail%20Story.pdf (14th Feb, 2009).
7   Union of Evangelical Students of India http://www.uesi.org.in/index.php?option=com_content&task=view&id=9&Itemid=31 (31st Aug 2007).
8   NA, *Witnesses for Me: A Manual for Evangelical Union* (Chennai: UESI, 1962), 9.
9   David Jayakumar, "Summary of Impact of UESI on Church, Missions and Society," (Manuscript of a presentation delivered at the UESI Golden Jubilee Conference, December, 2005), Jayakumar papers, UESI Archives, Hyderabad.
10 NA, *The Spreading Flame* (Madras: UESI Publication Trust, 1994), 12.
11 NA, *The Spreading Flame...*, 15.
12 Charles W. Doak, "The National Campus Ministry Association, 1964-94: A Brief History," *Journal of Ecumenical Studies* 32/4 (Fall 1995): 501.
13 H. Enoch, *Following the Master* (Mumbai: GLS, 1977), 72.
14 *Witnesses for Me- A Manual for Evangelical Union...*, 9.
15 P. Sathkeerthi Rao, "History of Union of Evangelical Students of India," (Manuscript of a presentation delivered at the UESI Golden Jubilee Conference, December, 2005), Sathkeerthi papers, UESI Archives, Hyderabad.
16 David Jayakumar, "Summary of Impact of UESI on Church, Missions and Society...*, 66.
17 J. H. Bavinck, *The Impact of Christianity on the Non-Christian World* (Michigan: Wm. B. Eerdmans Publishing Co, 1949), 55.
18 S. Wesley Ariarajah, *Gospel and Culture* (Thiruvalla: CSS, 1995), 3.
19 J. Mattam, "The message of Jesus and our customary theological language: An Indian approach to a new language in theology and inculturation," *Exchange* 34/3 (2005): 129.
20 M. D. David, "Indian Attitude towards Missionaries and their Work-With Special Reference to Maharastra," *Indian Church History Review* XXIX/2 (December, 1995), 94.
21 F. J. Balasundaram, "Gandhi's Attitude towards Christianity," *Indian Church History Review* XXVIII/1 (June 1994), 53.
22 David, "Indian Attitude towards Missionaries and their Work-With Special Reference to Maharastra...*, 94.
23 Y. Vincent Kumar Doss, "The Swadeshi Movement and the Attitude of the Protestant Christian Elite in Madras," *Indian Church History Review* XXXII/1 (June 1988), 15.

24 Doss, "The Swadeshi Movement and the Attitude of the protestant Christian Elite in Madras...", 15.
25 V.V Thomas, *Understanding Subaltern History: Theological Tools* (Bangalore: BTESSC/SATHRI, 2006), 48.
26 Mark Laing, "Mission by Education: An Examination of Alexander Duff's Missiological and its Outcome," *Bangalore Theological Forum* XXXIV/2 (December 2002), 209.
27 Ebenezer D. Dasan, *Contemporary issues related to contextualization in the light of Friends Missionary Prayer Band's ministry in South Gujarat from the beginning till present time* (M.Th Thesis, Senate of Serampore, 1999), 11.
28 Dasan, *The impact of the Gospel on the adivasis of South Gujarat: An investigation into the mission methods*, (PhD Dissertation, Consortium for Indian Missiological Education in collaboration with the Fuller University, Bangalore, 2006), 403.
29 Darrell L. Whiteman, "Contextualization: The Theory, the Gap, the Challenge," *International Bulletin of Missionary Research* 21/1 (January, 1997), 2.
30 Phil Parshall, *New Paths in Muslim Evangelism: Evangelical approaches to contextualization* (Michigan: Baker Book House, 1980), 31.
31 John Stringer, "Contextualization: Transformational Trialogue," *St Francis Magazine* 1/ III (June 2007): 1. http://www.stfrancismagazine.info/pdf/2007/june07-7.pdf (2nd October, 2008).
32 Paul G. Hiebert, *Anthropological insights for Missionaries* (Michigan: Baker Book House, 1985), 184.
33 Hiebert, *Anthropological insights for Missionaries*..., 184.
34 Paul G. Hiebert, "Critical Contextualization," *International Bulletin of Missionary Research* 11/3 (July, 1987), 111.
35 Ebenezer D. Dasan, "Holistic Contextualization," (Manuscript of a presentation delivered at the UBS Faculty Paper Presentation, October, 2007), 8. Dasan Papers, Union Biblical Seminary Archives, Pune.
36 Muslim colleges in India, http://www.milligazette.com/Archives/01-1-2000/Art7.htm (13th Nov, 2008).
37 John Mark Terry "Approaches to the evangelization of Muslims," *Evangelical Missions Quarterly* 23/2 (April 1996), 170.
38 Rick Brown, "The 'Son of God' Understanding the Messianic Titles of Jesus," *International Journal of Frontier Missions*, 17/1 (Spring 2000), 46.
39 Lyle Vander Werff, "Our Muslim Neighbors: The Contribution of Samuel M. Zwemer to Christian Mission," *Missiology* 10/2 (April 1982), 188.
40 Terry, "Approaches to the evangelization of Muslims...", 170.
41 Phil Parshall, "Muslim Evangelism: Mobilizing the national church," *Evangelical Missions Quarterly* 37/1 (January, 2001), 47.
42 Lyle L. Vander Werff, *Christian Mission to Muslims* (South Pasadena: William Carey Library, 1977), 61.
43 Terry, "Approaches to the Evangelization of Muslims," *Evangelical Missions Quarterly* ..., 170.

44 NA, "Mission and Evangelism: An Ecumenical Affirmation. Geneva: World Council of Churches, 1982," *International Review of Mission* 74/296 (Oct, 1985), 517.
45 Bernard Dutch, "Should Muslims Become Christians?" *International Journal of Frontier Missions*, 17/1 (Spring 2000), 15.
46 Stringer, "Contextualization: Transformational Trialogue," *St Francis Magazine...*, 4.
47 Jim Leffel, "Contextualization: Building Bridges to the Muslim Community," http://www.xenos.org/ministries/crossroads/OnlineJournal/issue1/contextu.htm#Note3 (2nd October, 2008).
48 Joshua Massey, "God's Amazing Diversity in Drawing Muslims to Christ," *International Journal of Frontier Missions*, 17/1 (Spring 2000), 5.
49 Ron Hutchcraft, "How to Communicate With Young People," in *The Mission of an Evangelist: Amsterdam 2000 A Conference of Preaching Evangelists*, edited by William W. Conard (Minneapolis: World Wide Publications, 2001), 301.
50 Phil Parshall, "Danger! New Directions in Contextualization," *Evangelical Missions Quarterly* 34 /4 (October 1998), 408.
51 Parshall, "Danger! New Directions in Contextualization," *Evangelical Missions Quarterly...*, 405.
52 Stringer, "Contextualization: Transformational Trialogue," *St Francis Magazine...*, 7.
53 Richard Jameson and Nick Scalevich, "First-Century Jews and Twentieth-Century Muslims," *International Journal of Frontier Missions*, 17/1 (Spring 2000), 35.
54 Massey, "God's Amazing Diversity in Drawing Muslims to Christ...", 8.
55 Parshall, "Danger! New Directions in Contextualization," *Evangelical Missions Quarterly...*, 409.
56 Timothy C. Tennent, "The Challenge of Churchless Christianity: An Evangelical Assessment," *International Bulletin of Missionary Research* 29/4 (O 2005), 171.
57 Brown, "Is planting churches in the Muslim World "Mission Impossible," *Evangelical Missions Quarterly* 33/2 (April 1997), 158.
58 John Travis, "Must all Muslims leave 'Islam' to follow Jesus," *Evangelical Missions Quarterly* 34 /4 (October 1998), 411.
59 Phil Parshall, Contextualized Baptism for Muslim Converts," *Missiology* 7/4 (October, 1979), 505.
60 Parshall, "Muslim Evangelism: Mobilizing the national church...", 45.
61 Parshall, "Muslim Evangelism: Mobilizing the national church...", 45.
62 T. A. Mathias, "The National Board of Christian Higher Education in India," *Religious Education* 63/1 (Jan-Feb 1968), 36.
63 H. L. Richard, "Evangelical Approaches to Hindus," *Missiology* 29/3 (July 2001), 307.

64 P.T. Abraham, "Pentecostal Charismatic Missionary Outreach," in *Proclaiming Christ: A Handbook of Indigenous Missions in India*, edited by Sam Lazarus (Madras: church growth Association of India, 1992), 103.
65 P. T. Chandi, "Christian Colleges and the India of Tomorrow," *Religious Education* 63/1 (Jan-Feb 1968), 40.
66 Eric J. Sharpe, "The Legacy of J. N. Farquhar," *Occasional Bulletin of Missionary Research* 3/2 (April, 1979), 63.
67 J. Gonda, "Vedic Gods and the sacrifice," *Numen* 32/1 (July 1985), 6.
68 Ravela Joseph, *Bhakti theology* (Chennai: Christian literature society, 2004), 72.
69 John Waliggo, "Inculturation," *Dictionary of the Ecumenical Movement*, edited by Nicholas Lossky (Grand Rapids: WCC Publications, 1991), 506.
70 Joseph Prasad Pinto, *Inculturation through Basic Community-An Indian Perspective* (New Delhi: F. M. Pais for the Asian Trading, 1985), 13.
71 Terry C.Muck, "Theology of Religions after Knitter and Hick: Beyond the Paradigm," *Interpretation* 61/1 (January, 2007), 19.
72 Samuel Rayan, "Inculturation and the Local Church, *"Mission Studies* 3/2 (1986), 15.
73 S. Venantius Fernando, "The Inculturation of the Church in India: A Controversy," *Missiology* 7/1 (Jan 1979), 107.
74 Donald McGavran, *Understanding Church Growth* (Grand Rapids: Eerdmans, 1970), 198.
75 Victor Hayward and Donald McGavran, "Without crossing barriers: One in Christ vs. discipling diverse cultures," *Missiology* 2/2 (April 1974), 203.
76 Ebe Sunder Raj, *Sat Guru Aradhana* (Mussoorie: Nivedit Good Books, 2007), 12.
77 Jack C. Winslow, *The Christian approach to the Hindu* (Edinburgh: Morrison and Gibb Limited, 1958), 38.
78 Y. Vincent Kumaradoss, "Creation of alternative Public spheres and church indigenization in nineteenth century colonial Tamil Nadu: The Hindu-Christian church of Lord Jesus and the National Church of India," in *Christianity is Indian: The Emergence of an indigenous community*, edited by Roger E. Hedlund (Delhi: ISPCK, 2000), 10.
79 Dasan Jeyaraj, "Followers of Christ outside the Church and Missiological Education," A paper presented at the CMS Consultation, UBS, Pune on 17th January, 2007), 17.
80 S. Wesley Ariarajah, "Witness to Hindu Neighbors," *International Review of Mission* 72/285 (Jan 1983), 86.
81 Herbert E. Hoefer, *Churchless Christianity* (California: William Carey Library, 1999), 157.
82 Jeyaraj, "Followers of Christ outside the Church and Missiological Education…, 17.
83 Tennent, "The Challenge of Churchless Christianity: An Evangelical Assessment…, 171.

84 Sunder Raj, *Sat Guru Aradhana...*, 31.
85 H. L. Richard, *Exploring the depths of the mystery of Christ: K. Subba Rao's eclectic praxis of Hindu Discipleship to Jesus* (Bangalore: Centre for contemporary Christianity, 2005), 147.
86 M. Stephen, *A Christian theology in the Indian context* (Delhi: ISPCK, 2005), 26.
87 Hiebert, *Anthropological Insights for Missionaries...*, 185.
88 Moses Premanandham, "God-Chosen Movement for India," in *Christianity is Indian...*, 344.
89 George David, "Mission to Hindus," in *Proclaiming Christ*, edited by Sam Lazarus (Madras: Church Growth Association of India, 1992), 45.
90 David, "Mission to Hindus," in *Proclaiming Christ...*, 46.
91 Satish Simon, "History of UESI," (Manuscript of a presentation delivered at the Committee Members Training Camp, June 2005), Simon Papers, UESI Archives, Delhi.
92 Daniel I. Leifer, "A Ministry to Students: A Symposium on Current Concerns in Campus Ministry," *Christian Century* 96/33 (Oct 17, 1979), 1002
93 Sabin P. Landry, "Christian Ministry to the Campus in Historical Perspective," *Review & Expositor* 69/3 (Sum 1972), 311.
94 Paul Schrading, "A New Campus Ministry," *Theology Today* 26/4 (Jan 1970), 471.
95 B. K. Tettey, "Reflections on a ministry among students," *International Review of Mission* 66/262 (April 1977), 146.
96 Wayne C. Olson, "Campus Ministry as Remedial Religion," *Christian Century* 105/12 (April 13, 1988), 382.
97 Sanjay Seth, "Which good Book? Missionary education and conversion in colonial India," *Semeia* 88 (2001), 118.
98 Mithra G. Augustine, "Academic Apostolate in India," *Ecumenical Review* 30/1 (Jan, 1978), 51.
99 T. A. Mathias, "The National Board of Christian Higher Education in India," *Religious Education* 63/1 (Jan-Feb 1968): 38.
100 Augustine, "Academic Apostolate in India," *Ecumenical Review...*, 51.
101 Lucy Forster-Smith, "Musings on my Ministry," *Theology Today* 41/2 (July 1984), 181.
102 B.R. Mushota, Kasama and Zambia, "The Chaplaincies II in Hospitals, Secondary Schools and Universities," *AFER* 16/1 (January-April, 1974), 253.
103 Marie Susanne Hoffman, "Christian vision in academe," *Theology Today* 41/2 (July 1984), 190.
104 Karin Thornton, "Interfaith Worship on Campus," *Cross Currents* 40/1 (Spring, 1990), 27.
105 International Student Ministry, http://isminc.org/Home/tabid/613/Default.aspx (2nd Dec 2008).
106 John D. Lottes, "Jesus as Mentor: Biblical Reflections for Ministry with Young Adults," *Currents in Theology and Mission* 32/2 (April 2005), 128.

107 Sharon Daloz Parks, "Social Vision and Moral Courage: Mentoring a New Generation," *Cross Currents* 40/3 (Fall 1990), 357.
108 John D. Lottes, "Toward a Christian Theology of Hospitality to Other Religions on Campus," *Currents in Theology and Mission* 32/1 (Fall 2005), 27.
109 Hubert C. Noble, "Evangelism on the college campus," *Theology Today* 11/1 (April 1954), 64.
110 Noble, "Evangelism on the college campus…, 68.
111 Elizabeth Dreyer and Keith J. Egan, "Creative teaching: Christian prayer, practice and theory," *Horizons* 6/1 (Spring, 1979), 104.
112 John D. Perry, "The Coffee House Ministry," *Christian Century* 82/6 (F 10 1965), 181.
113 Hasan al-Ghazali, "In Coffee Houses," in *Muslims and Christians on the Emmaus Road*, edited by J. Dudley Woodberry (California: MARC, 1989), 197.
114 Hasan al-Ghazali, "In Coffee Houses," in *Muslims and Christians on the Emmaus Road…*, 199.
115 Jacob G. Isaac, "Making Difference among the Youth in India," *Indian Missions* 206/1(1st January 2006), 34.
116 Interview with M. Anil Kumar at his hostel room in Osmania University, Hyderabad on 19th May, 2008.
117 Interview with Dr. John Paul at his residence in Hyderabad on 25th May, 2008.
118 Interview with Rev. M. Sudhakar at his office in Hyderabad on 25th May 2008.
119 Interview with Mr. K. Ezekiel at office, APGENCO, in Hyderabad on 24th May, 2008.
120 Interview with Dr. Rathaiah in Hyderabad Central University Campus on 29th May 2008.
121 Interview with Dr. R. Daniel in JNTU campus of Hyderabad on 24th May 2008.
122 Interview with Mr. Emmanuel Subhakar at Hyderabad UESI City Office on 26th May 2008.
123 Interview with M. Anil Kumar at his hostel room in Osmania University, Hyderabad on 19th May, 2008.
124 Interview with Dr. John Paul at his residence in Hyderabad on 25th May, 2008.
125 Vikram P. Vardhan, Annual Executive Secretary Report to the UESI-AP AGM, 2008.
126 Interview with Mr. M. Sudhakar at his office in Hyderabad on 25th May 2008.
127 UESI, St. Anne's Generalate, Secunderabad, Minutes of the Annual General Body Meeting, 27-29 July 2007. 14. (Xeroxed).
128 Interview with Subash at his residence in Warangal on 14th May, 2008.

129 Interview with Dr. Sudheer Premkumar at his residence in JNTU Campus, Hyderabad on 29th May 2008.
130 Interview with B. Dayakar at his room in Hyderabad on 18th May 2008.
131 Interview with Dr. John Paul at his residence in Hyderabad on 25th May, 2008.
132 Interview with Mr. Emmanuel Subhakar at Hyderabad UESI City Office on 26th May 2008.
133 Interview with C. Chandra Shakar at his Hostel Room in Hyderabad Central University on 22nd May 2008.
134 Roger E. Hedlund, "Comments of Thesis," (27th Feb, 2009), Personal Email to the author (28th Nov 2009).
135 Interview with B. Dayakar at his room in Hyderabad on 18th May 2008.
136 Interview with B. Dayakar at his room in Hyderabad on 18th May 2008.
137 Interview with Mr. P. Vikram Vardhan at UESI City office in Hyderabad on 25th May 2008.
138 Interview with Mr. K. Ezekiel at his office, APGENCO, in Hyderabad on 24th May, 2008.
139 Interview with Mr. Dayanand at his residence in Hyderabad on 30th May 2008
140 Interview with Muntaj in Andhra University Campus in Vishakhapatnam on 30th April, 2008.
141 Joe L. Coker, "Developing a Theory of Mission in Serampore: The Increased Emphasis upon Education as a 'Means for the Conversion of the Heathens,'" *Mission Studies* 18/1 (2001), 42.
142 F. Deaville Walker, *William Carey* (Chicago: Moody Press, 1960), 175.
143 Steven M. Baugh, "Introduction To The Letter of Paul to the Ephesians," http://www.boundless.org/2005/articles/a0001865.cfm (12th Feb, 2009).
144 Interview with Mr. M. Sudhakar at his office in Hyderabad on 25th May 2008.
145 Dane Winstead Fowlkes, "Developing a Church planting movement in India" (PhD dissertation, University of the Free State, Bloemfontein, South Africa, November 2004). http://etd.uovs.ac.za/ETD-db//theses/available/etd-08222005-105223/unrestricted/FOWLKESDW.pdf (16th Feb 2009).
146 H. L. Richard, "A Survey of Protestant Evangelistic Efforts among High Caste Hindus in the Twentieth Century," *Missiology* 25/4 (October 1997): 424, citing J. Z. Hodge, "Forward Movement in Evangelism under the N.C.C," in *Evangelism* Vol. III (New York: International Missionary Council, 1939), 80.
147 NA, "Enhancements to Inductive Bible Study," InterVarsity/USA Bible Study Task Force-featured paper, April, 1999, http://www.intervarsity.org/biblestu/communal/enhancements_to_ibs.pdf (Jan 13, 2009).
148 Edward D. Seely, "Where Reformed Theology Meets and Shapes Youth Ministry: Facilitating Answers to Adolescents' Great Questions of life," *Calvin Theological Journal* 41/2 (N0v 2006), 332.

149 Interview with Mr. P. Vikram Vardhan at UESI City office in Hyderabad on 25th May 2008.
150 Interview with Mr. P. Vikram Vardhan at UESI City office in Hyderabad on 25th May 2008.
151 Interview with Mr. P. Vikram Vardhan at UESI City office in Hyderabad on 25th May 2008.
152 Interview with Dr. John Paul at his residence in Hyderabad on 25th May, 2008.
153 Interview with B. Dayakar at his room in Hyderabad on 18th May 2008.
154 Interview with Bhimalingam Chittari at his room in Hyderabad Central University on 22nd May 2008.
155 Interview with Muntaj Begam at Andhra University campus in Vishakapatnam on 30th April 2008.
156 Interview with B. Dayakar at his room in Hyderabad on 18th May 2008.
157 Interview with Ch. Bapuji at his residence in Hyderabad on 22nd May 2008.
158 Atul Y. Aghamkar, *Insights into openness: Encouraging urban mission* (Bangalore. SAIACS Press, 2000), 149.
159 Aghamkar, *Insights into openness...*, 89.
160 Frampton F. Fox, *Motivational factors among indigenous missionaries in India with special reference to the Friends Missionary Prayer Band* (D. Min Dissertation, Columbia Biblical Seminary and School of Missions, Columbia, May 2000), 3.
161 Arokiaraj Cosmon, " Catholic leader says Orissa quickly becoming saffronized," http://indianchristians.in/news/index2.php?option=com_content&do_pdf=1&id=1914 (2nd Feb, 2009).
162 Vatsala Vedantam, "Privilege and resentment: Religious conflict in India," *Christian Century* 116/12 (April, 14 1999), 415.
163 Donald McGavran, *Understanding Church Growth* (Grand Rapids: Eerdmans, 1970), 198.
164 Paul G. Hiebert, "Critical Contextualization," *International Bulletin of Missionary Research* 11/3 (July, 1987): 111.
165 Roger E. Hedlund, *Quest for Identity* (New Delhi: ISPCK, 2000), 48.
166 Atulkumar Yeshwantrao Aghamkar, *Approaching Urban Hindus: A study of Christian approaches and Hindu responses in Pune City, India*, (PhD Dissertation, Fuller Theological Seminary, California, May 1995), 145.
167 Hedlund, *Quest for Identity...*, 48.
168 Interview with Mr. P. Vikram Vardhan at UESI City office in Hyderabad on 25th May 2008.
169 Interview with Mr. Emmanuel Subhakar at Hyderabad UESI City Office on 26th May 2008.
170 Interview with Dr. R. Daniel in JNTU campus of Hyderabad on 24th May 2008.
171 Interview with Dr. R. Daniel in JNTU campus of Hyderabad on 24th May 2008.
172 Interview with Mr. B.V.L.R.Prasad over the telephone on 11th Feb, 2009.

173 Interview with R. Srinivasa Rao at UBS, Pune, during his stay for his M.Div contact classes on 11th Feb, 2009.
174 Interview with Mr. P. Vikram Vardhan over the telephone on 11th Feb, 2009.
175 Interview with Mr. B.V.L.R.Rrasad over the telephone on 11th Feb, 2009.
176 Interview with Mr. M. Sudhakar at his office in Hyderabad on 27th May 2008.
177 Interview with Mr. K. Sudhakar Rao at his office in Nambur, Guntur on 25th April, 2008.
178 Interview with B. Dayakar at his room in Hyderabad on 18th May 2008.
179 Interview with Muntaj Begam at Andhra University campus in Vishakapatnam on 30th April 2008.
180 Interview with Ibrahim at Andhra University in Vishakapatnam on 30th April 2008.
181 Interview with Muntaj Begam at Andhra University campus in Vishakapatnam on 30th April 2008.
182 Raju has answered the questionnaire Mission among students of different faiths related to the programs for students of different faiths on the 18th May 2008 from Hyderabad.
183 B. Raju has answered the questionnaire the ministry of UESI to friends from different faiths in Hyderabad Universities on 12th May 2008.
184 Rahmatulla has answered the questionnaire the ministry of UESI to friends from different faiths in Hyderabad Universities on 25th May 2008.
185 Divakar Reddy has answered the questionnaire the ministry of UESI to friends from different faiths in Hyderabad Universities on 25th May 2008.
186 R. Sugunakar has answered the questionnaire the ministry of UESI to friends from different faiths in Hyderabad Universities on 19th May 2008.
187 Interview with Mr. P. Vikram Vardhan at UESI City office in Hyderabad on 25th May 2008.
188 Interview with Dr. R. Daniel in JNTU campus of Hyderabad on 24th May 2008.
189 Interview with Mr. P. Vikram Vardhan at UESI City office in Hyderabad on 25th May 2008.
190 Interview with C. Chandra Shakar at his Hostel Room in Hyderabad Central University on 22nd May 2008.
191 Vikram P. Vardhan, "Executive Secretary Report," AGM 2008 9TH-11TH May '08, 45.
192 Interview with Mr. M. Sudhakar at his office in Hyderabad on 25th May 2008.
193 Interview with Dr. R. Daniel in JNTU campus of Hyderabad on 24th May 2008.
194 Tina Thomas, et al., "CMTC-2006," UESI in Touch IX/8 (August 2006), 4.
195 Interview with Mr. P. Vikram Vardhan at UESI City office in Hyderabad on 25th May 2008.

196 Interview with Dr. John Paul at his residence in Hyderabad on 25th May, 2008.
197 Interview with Mr. K. Ezekiel at office, APGENCO, in Hyderabad on 24th May, 2008.
198 Interview with Muntaj Begam at Andhra University campus in Vishakapatnam on 30th April 2008.
199 Interview with Mr. K. Sudhakar Rao at his office in Nambur, Guntur on 25th April, 2008.
200 NA, Indian population, http://www.iloveindia.com/population-of-india/index.html (14th Jan, 2009).
201 Jacob G. Isaac, "Making Difference among the Youth in India," *Indian Missions* 206/1(1st January 2006): 34.
202 Parshall, *New Paths in Muslim Evangelism...*, 31.
203 George Verwer, *Literature Evang*elism (Chicago: Moody Press, 1963), 10.
204 Aghamkar, *Insights into openness...*, 163.
205 Parshall, "Danger! New Directions in Contextualization," *Evangelical Missions Quarterly...*, 405.
206 UESI, St. Anne's Generalate, Secunderabad, Minutes of the Annual General Body Meeting..., 14.
207 A. Vijaya Kumar has answered the questionnaire Mission among students of different faiths related to the possible hindrances to share the Gospel to Hindu background students on the 10th May 2008 from Hyderabad.
208 U. David Jaya Kumar, "Scaling Different Heights," in Glow for God UESI-AP TRICON 2006, 39. (Seminary paper).
209 Satish has answered the questionnaire Mission among students of different faiths related to the possible hindrances to share the Gospel to Hindu background students on the 10th May 2008 from Hyderabad., questionnaire
210 Interview with Mr. M. Sudhakar at his office in Hyderabad on 25th May 2008.
211 Interview with Mr. K. Ezekiel at office, APGENCO, in Hyderabad on 24th May, 2008.
212 Interview with SK. Emmanuel Pasha at Word and Deed in Hyderabad on 17th May 2008.
213 Rama Madhuri has answered the questionnaire Mission among students of different faiths related to the possible hindrances to share the Gospel to Christian background students on the 20th May 2008 from Hyderabad.
214 U. David Jaya Kumar, "Scaling Different Heights," in Glow for God UESI-AP TRICON 2006, 39. (Seminary paper).
215 Mondithoka Sudhakar, "Answering the Skeptics: Equipping Ourselves for Evangelism," in Glow for God UESI-AP TRICON 2006, 46. (Seminary paper).
216 Tina Thomas, Howard Wodomal, Bejoy John & Sathish Joseph Simon, "CMTC-2006," *UESI in Touch* IX/8 (August 2006), 1. (1-6).

217 Interview with Mr. Emmanuel Subhakar at Hyderabad UESI City Office on 26th May 2008.
218 Interview with Mr. M. Sudhakar at his office in Hyderabad on 25th May 2008.
219 UESI, St. Anne's Generalate, Secunderabad, Minutes of the Annual General Body Meeting... 14.
220 Interview with Mr. M. Sudhakar at his office in Hyderabad on 25th May 2008.
221 Interview with Muntaj Begam at Andhra University campus in Vishakapatnam on 30th April 2008.
222 "Closed room dialogues" means a few Muslims and Christians come together to discuss and clarify their religious arguments in a room/house or a hotel where there is only a small group.
223 Interview with Mr. M. Sudhakar at his office in Hyderabad on 25th May 2008.
224 "1:3 Discipling" means each EGF member in every city is assigned one senior EU student and one fresh student who accepted the Lord. They function like a micro cell group in which they meet frequently for prayer and fellowship apart from the regular Bible studies and programs. The purpose of this micro cell is to mentor the students.
225 Interview with Mr. K. Sudhakar Rao at his office in Nambur, Guntur on 25th April, 2008.
226 G. Krishna Reddy has answered the questionnaire Mission among students of different faiths related to the needed follow-up to Christian background students on the 25th May 2008 from Hyderabad.
227 G. Rajesh Babu has answered the questionnaire Mission among students of different faiths related to the needed follow-up to Christian background students on the 25th May 2008 from Hyderabad.
228 Interview with Ibrahim at Andhra University in Vishakapatnam on 30th April 2008.
229 David Schmidt, "Developing a Heart for Lost People in an Apathetic Church," in *The Mission of an Evangelist: Amsterdam 2000 A Conference of Preaching Evangelists*, edited by William W. Conard (Minneapolis: World Wide Publications, 2001), 323.
230 K. P. Yohannan, "A Bringing Our Hearts into Focus," in *Perspectives: On World Missions South Asia Version* (Bangalore: New Life Literature, 1998), 2.
231 David Walling, *Witnessing the Gospel to the immigrant Muslims in Nagaland*, (B.D Thesis, Union Biblical Seminary, Pune, March 200), 29.
232 Michael Nazir-Ali, *Mission and Dialogue: Proclaiming the Gospel afresh in every age* (London: SPCK, 1995), 83.
233 Roger Chilvers, "Personal Evangelism and Counselor Training," in *The Mission of an Evangelist: Amsterdam 2000 A Conference of Preaching Evangelists*, edited by William W. Conard (Minneapolis: World Wide Publications, 2001), 202.

234 Phil and Marion Grasham, "Ministry among the Fulbe," *International Journal of Frontier Missions* 17/3 (Fall 2000), 29.
235 Steve Clapp and Sam Detwiler, *Sharing living water: Evangelism as caring friendship* (Illinois: Brethren Press, 2000), 101.
236 Sami Dagher, "The Evangelist Is Faithful in a Hostile World," in *The Mission of an Evangelist: Amsterdam 2000 A Conference of Preaching Evangelists*, edited by William W. Conard (Minneapolis: World Wide Publications, 2001), 273.
237 Sami Dagher, "The Evangelist Is Faithful in a Hostile World," in *The Mission of an Evangelist: Amsterdam 2000 A Conference of Preaching Evangelists*, edited by William W. Conard (Minneapolis: World Wide Publications, 2001), 273.
238 John Travis, "Messianic Muslim Followers of *Isa:* A Closer Look at C5 Believers and Congregations," *International Journal of Frontier Missions* 17/1 (Spring 2000), 53-59.
239 A. Scott Moreau, "Mission and Missions," in *Evangelical Dictionary of World Missions*, edited by A. Scott Moreau (Michigan: Baker Books, 2000), 636.
240 Arthur F. Glasser, A*nnouncing the Kingdom* (Michigan: Baker Academic, 2003), 56.
241 H. Cornell Goerner, *All Nations in God's Purpose* (Nashville: Bradman Press, 1979), 22
242 Roger E. Hedlund, *God and the Nations: a Biblical Theology of Mission in the Asian Context* (Delhi: ISPCK, 1997), 61.
243 Veli-Matti Kärkkäinen, *An introduction to the Theology of Religions* (Illinois: InterVarsity Press, 2003), 44.
244 F. C. Beicho, *The Missionary methods of the Evangelical Church of Maraland among the Tiwa tribes of Assam,* (M.Th Thesis, Union Biblical Seminary, Pune, March 2006), 79.
245 Interview with B. Dayakar at his room in Hyderabad on 18th May 2008.
246 Matured believing students who have concern for mission work and willing to go to unreached universities to establish students' ministry through their presence. Instead of doing courses in their own place, they join in unreached universities.

Index

A
Alexander Duff 14, 35
Andhra Pradesh 6-7, 12, 30, 47, 55, 98
Apologetic/s 18-19

B
Bakht Singh 12, 33
Balanced Contextualization 22-23
Baptism 25-26, 33
Bhakti Tradition 32-34
Bible 12, 22, 24, 34, 50-52, 79, 83, 90
Bible Study/ies 7, 21, 39, 41, 45-46, 48-51, 57, 74-75, 82-84, 91, 93
Bramhobandha Upadhyaya 32
British Colonies 21
British Imperialism 14

C
Campus Ministry/ies 2, 12, 18-19, 27, 37, 39, 41
Chaplaincy 36
Chekkraiah 32
Christian 1-5, 11, 13-25, 28-37, 41, 43-44, 47, 50, 52-61, 63-85, 87, 90-92, 96-99
Christian Culture 21-22, 30, 92, 97
Christian Witness 37, 44, 51, 97, 99
Christianity 13-15, 23, 29-31, 35, 54-57, 61, 79
Christmas Programs 47, 49
Church 1-3, 12-15, 18-19, 21-26, 29-33, 35-36, 39-40, 50-51, 53, 56, 60, 66, 69-71, 75-77, 87, 90, 92, 94, 99
Churchless Christianity 31-32
Coffee House 39-41, 76
Confrontational Method 18
Contextual Approach 13, 16-17, 20, 22, 30-31, 40-41, 51, 56-57, 76-77, 88
Contextualization 12, 15-16, 20, 22-23, 29-30, 40, 76
Critical Contextualization 17, 40, 57
Cross-Cultural Mission 15
Cultural Context 13, 15, 22, 27, 30-31

D
Dalits 1, 30, 56, 61
Dan Brown 24
Dasan Jeyaraj 32
David Jaya Kumar 3, 13, 81
Dayanand Bharati 16, 32-33
Dialogical Approach 19-20

Index

Different Faiths 35-40, 44-45, 47, 49, 52, 54, 56-64, 72-78, 88, 94-95, 98

E

Ebe Sunder Raj 30
Evangelical 12, 18-20, 27, 40-41, 50
Exegesis of the Culture 17

F

Follow-up 67-68, 76
Fulfillment Theory 28

G

General Approaches 12-15

H

High-caste Hindus 1, 3, 13, 30, 57, 92, 97, 99
Hindu/s 1-5, 11, 14, 16, 26-33, 37, 41, 43-44, 52-79, 81-87, 89-99
Hindu Theology 1
Hindu-Christian 31
Hoefer 32
Holistic Mission 17
Homogenous Unit Principle 30
Hospitality 37-38, 41, 76, 94

I

Inculturation 29-30, 33
Indian Context 12, 15, 33, 36, 77
Indigenization 15
Indigenous 12-13, 22, 25, 29, 32-33, 40, 99
Indigenous Language 21-22
Insider View 23-24, 31
Institutional Approach 19
Interfaith Worship 36-37
Islam 16, 18-19

J

John Mark Terry 18

L

Lord's Supper 31

M

Messianic Jews 23
Messianic Mosques 23
Missiological Education 32
Missionary/ies 3-4, 13-18, 20-22, 25-26, 28, 34-36, 39-40, 50, 57, 69, 77, 89, 92, 97-98
Mission/s 1-5, 8, 13, 15-23, 26-31, 33-41, 44, 50-52, 57, 76, 88-91, 95, 98-99
Mosque 23-24
Multi-religious 13
Muslim 1-5, 11-12, 15-26, 30, 32, 37-41, 43-44, 49-50, 52-58, 61-80, 82-99
Muslim-background Believer 22, 25-26

N

Narayan Vaman Tilak 32
Nehemiah Goreh 29
Non-approach 27
Non-contextualization 21

O

Orthodox Church 21
Outreach 15, 20, 22, 52, 77, 83, 88

P

Parshall 15, 22-23, 26, 77
Paul G. Hiebert 1, 16
Pavitra Prasad 31
Pentecostal 27-28
Personal Evangelism 38-39, 41, 45-47, 49-51, 81-83, 87, 92
Pluralistic 15, 36, 79
Ponnuraj 12
Pragmatic Approaches 27-28
Prajapati 28
Proclamation 19-20, 37-38
Professor Enoch 12, 40

R

R.C. Das 16
Rajendra B. Lal 32

Rejection of Contextualization 16
Richard 27, 29, 41, 51

S

Sadhu Sunder Singh 16
Salvation 12, 46, 90
Samuel Zwemer 18
Sangh Parivar 26
Sattampillai 31
Secret Followers 24
Self Baptism 25
Simple Gospel Approach 27
Social service 19, 35
Society 1-3, 13-14, 19, 34-35, 39, 56, 69, 71-72, 76-77, 87, 94
Student Christian Movement 12, 34, 44
Student Ministry 11, 34
Student Movement 2-4, 12-13, 34-35, 40, 44, 56, 91
Subba Rao 32-33

T

Theological Education Fund 15
Tract Distribution 48
Traditional 18-19, 21, 26-27, 29, 32-33, 40, 44, 46, 49-50, 57, 76, 83, 86, 91, 96
Transformation 38, 58

U

Uncritical Contextualization 16, 33, 40
University Students 16, 19-22, 29, 32, 34, 37-38, 46, 51, 89
Upadhyaya, 16, 32

V

Visakhapatnam 12

W

Western Approach 19
Western Missionaries 13-14, 21, 40, 50
Word of God 12, 18

Y

Yesu Darbar 32